On Becoming
A Disciple-
Scholar

D1603310

On Becoming A Disciple-Scholar

Lectures Presented at the
Brigham Young University Honors Program
Discipline and Discipleship Lecture Series

EDITED BY HENRY B. EYRING

Bookcraft
Salt Lake City, Utah

Contents

Preface

These lectures were presented to students in the Brigham Young University Honors Program during 1994 and 1995 in the intimate setting of the Coray Lecture Hall of the historic Karl G. Maeser Building, the oldest building on the Brigham Young University campus. An additional lecture presented at the annual Honors Program banquet is also included.

The primary goal of the BYU Honors Program is to model the compatibility of rigorous scholarship with deep devotion to the faith, including institutional aspects of the faith. The lecturers in the Discipline and Discipleship lecture series were invited to explore the relationship between secular studies in the various academic disciplines and the personal development of religious commitment requisite to true discipleship.

What emerged from the lectures was a portrait of the disciple-scholar, students or scholars who seek to prepare to serve God through their studies.

It is hoped that these lectures will prove useful to Latter-day Saint students wherever they may be, as well as to students of other faiths who seek to enrich their secular studies through their religious commitment.

1

ELDER NEAL A. MAXWELL

The Disciple-Scholar

I thank Dean Paul Cox and those associated with him for their spiritual vision of the Honors Program at Brigham Young University. Dean Cox not only is a world-class scholar but has a world-class testimony, too.

I commend your having among your readings Stephen Carter's book *The Culture of Disbelief,* since, of necessity, you will function in that challenging culture in the years ahead.

Not long after I became Commissioner of Church Education, way back in 1970, I asked if I might briefly teach an honors class at BYU. I had been teaching an honors class at the University of Utah on American political ideas and wanted to see how the "U" and the "Y" students compared. I found what I expected—that the BYU students were every bit as bright and enjoyable as were the students at the University of Utah. There was only one difference: at a state university, and quite properly, I could not inject gospel concepts into my teaching, such as pertained to the nature of man and therefore to what kind of government is best for man, and so forth. This may seem a small point, but in fact the opportunity for the infusion of gospel concepts confers a major advantage associated with being a disciple-scholar of which there will be some illustrations to follow.

Honorable Individuals: Commendable but Not Celestial

You are in the Honors Program because of your merit and unusual capacity. This is significant, and so is the word *honor.* I call your attention, however, to the scripture which describes the terrestrial kingdom as including the honorable individuals of the earth. What so many honorable individuals do is certainly useful and even commendable. But their focus is not on the celestial, and hence they may be "taken in" by the world and are not "valiant in the testimony of Jesus." (D&C 76:75, 79.)

Given all of your talents and opportunities, I hope you will not settle for being among the "honorable" men and women of the earth. Furthermore, along with your many gifts and talents, you have been given much; hence much is "required" (D&C 82:3). The word is *required,* not the words "hoped for," "expected," or the phrase "it would be nice if . . ."

This is a time in your lives when you are blossoming and stretching. My regard is for what you now are, but also for what you have the power to become. This causes me to speak to you of overarching and undergirding things. For instance, the distinguishing and facilitating quality of meekness will be noted more than once in these remarks. How you treat those *around* you, *below* you, and *behind* you in life will matter greatly in your lives.

No Conflict Between Faith and Learning

The Lord sees no conflict between faith and learning in a broad curriculum:

> . . . that you may be instructed more perfectly in theory, in principle, in doctrine, in the law of the gospel, in all things that pertain unto the kingdom of God, that are expedient for you to understand;
> Of things both in heaven and in earth, and under the earth; things which have been, things which are, things which must shortly come to pass; things which are at home, things which are abroad; the wars and the perplexities of the nations, and the judgments which are on the land; and a knowledge also of countries and of kingdoms. . . .
> And as all have not faith, seek ye diligently and teach one another words of wisdom; yea, seek ye out of the best books words of wisdom; seek learning even by study and also by faith. (D&C 88:78–79, 118.)

The scriptures see faith and learning as mutually facilitating, not separate processes. Robert Frost's line "Something there is that doesn't love a wall" is applicable regarding a wall between mind and spirit.

Are All Truths of Equal Importance?

Since truth is highly and rightly valued in the learning process, please allow me to present a few graphic illustrations about the gradations of truth. These points may seem obvious, but it is so easy to look "beyond the mark" (Jacob 4:14).

The restored gospel of Jesus Christ gives us a different view of truth. To begin with, there is no democracy among truths. They are not of equal significance. These gradations might be represented geometrically by a wide circle (see figure 1).

Gradations of Truth

There is no democracy among truths

Figure 1

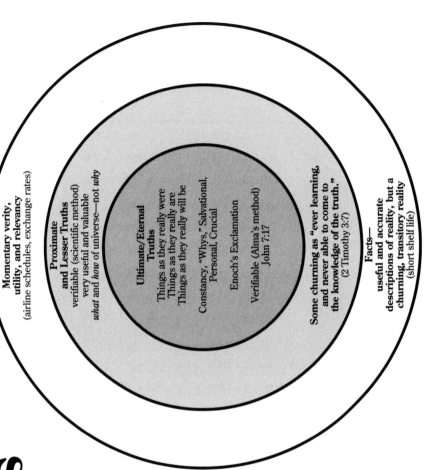

Momentary verity, utility, and relevancy
(airline schedules, exchange rates)

Proximate and Lesser Truths
verifiable (scientific method)
very useful and valuable
what and *how* of universe—not *why*

Ultimate/Eternal Truths
Things as they really were
Things as they really are
Things as they really will be

Constancy, "Whys," Salvational,
Personal, Crucial

Enoch's Exclamation

Verifiable (Alma's method)
John 7:17

Some churning as "ever learning,
and never able to come to
the knowledge of the truth."
(2 Timothy 3:7)

Facts—
useful and accurate
descriptions of reality, but a
churning, transitory reality
(short shelf life)

The outer edges of the circle would include truths which are accurate descriptions of reality. These facts, such as airline schedules and exchange rates, have only a momentary utility and relevancy, a short shelf life. They are useful, and they cannot be ignored, but they are simply not on the same footing as other kinds of truth. You could supply your own and better illustrations.

The next concentric circle inward (figure 1) would include more important truths. These are proximate and important truths, however, not ultimate truths. Some of these, for instance, are verifiable by the very serviceable scientific method. These truths can be very useful and valuable. For instance, in the realm of astrophysics they tell us much about the *what* and *how* of the universe, but they cannot (and do not even presume to) tell us *why* it exists.

In this same middle circle, the suburbs, so to speak, there is a churning and revising among some of these truths. Life in the suburbs may mean one can be "ever learning" but still "never able to come to a knowledge of *the* truth" (2 Timothy 3:7). Even so, these truths are important and valued.

In the very center of the circle of truth (figure 1) lie the "deep things of God" (1 Corinthians 2:10, 14). These come to us only by revelation from God, and they clearly have a greater significance than other truths and fleeting facts.

These truths concern things as they really were, really are, and really will be (D&C 93:24). There is constancy, not churning, among these strategic truths. These truths, for instance, are revealed from God and tell us *why* the universe exists. They are also very personal and crucial, such as is contained in Enoch's exclamation (see Moses 7:30). They represent the highest order of truth.

These truths are likewise verifiable. Jesus describes how: "If any man will do his will, he shall know of the doctrine, whether it be of God, or whether I speak of myself" (John 7:17; see also Alma 32:26–43).

Prioritizing Truths

Thus we constantly need to distinguish between the truths which are useful and those which are crucial, and between truths which are important and those which are eternal. The restored gospel gives us this special sense of proportion.

Stephen Hawking, displaying that meekness which is found in great scientists, wrote: "Although science may solve the problem of how the universe began, it cannot answer the question: Why does the universe bother to exist? I don't know the answer to that." (Stephen W. Hawking, *Black Holes and Baby Universes* [New York: Bantam Books, 1993], p. 99.)

Hawking also raised some ultimate questions pertaining to the innermost zone of figure 1. He wrote:

> What is the nature of the universe? What is our place in it and where did it and we come from? Why is it the way it is? . . .
> . . . If we do discover a complete theory, . . . then we shall all . . . be able to take part in the discussion of the question of why it is that we and the universe exist. If we find the answer to that, it would be the ultimate triumph of human reason—for then we would know the mind of God. (Stephen W. Hawking, *A Brief History of Time* [New York: Bantam Books, 1988], pp. 171, 175.)

Such questions are answered only by revelation, not solely by reason. Certain high-grade knowledge, as Paul taught, is "spiritually discerned" (1 Corinthians 2:14). Only when mind and spirit combine can we penetrate the inner realm.

Nephi lamented over those who "will not search knowledge, nor understand great knowledge" (2 Nephi 32:7). Clearly he was referring to a particular gradation of knowledge. Jesus lamented that some had lost the "key of knowledge." Joseph Smith translated the word *key* as "the fulness of the scriptures" (JST Luke 11:53; see also D&C 84:19–20).

Yes, we are nourished in many helpful ways by certain facts and feelings, but as Jacques Maritain observed: "Poetry (like metaphysics) is spiritual nourishment; but of a savor which has been created and which is insufficient. There is but

one eternal nourishment. Unhappy are you who think yourselves ambitious, and who whet your appetites for anything
less than the [divinity] of Christ. It is a mortal error to expect
from poetry the super-substantial nourishment of man."
(Jacques Maritain, *Frontiers of Poetry* [New York: Charles
Scribner's Sons, 1962], p. 132.)

Scholarship as a Form of Worship

For a disciple of Jesus Christ, academic scholarship is a
form of worship. It is actually another dimension of consecration. Hence one who seeks to be a disciple-scholar will take
both scholarship and discipleship seriously; and, likewise,
gospel covenants. For the disciple-scholar, the first and second
great commandments frame and prioritize life. How else could
one worship God with all of one's heart, might, *mind*, and
strength? (Luke 10:27.) Adoration of God leads to emulation of
Him and Jesus: "Therefore, what manner of men ought ye to
be? Verily I say unto you, even as I am." (3 Nephi 27:27; see
also 2 Peter 3:11.)

So much tutoring is required, however, in order for the disciple to become "as a child, submissive, meek, humble,
patient, full of love, willing to submit to all things which the
Lord seeth fit to inflict upon him, even as a child doth submit
to his father" (Mosiah 3:19).

The disciple-scholar also understands what kind of community he or she should help to build. Its citizens openly and genuinely desire to be called God's people. They are not secret disciples, but bear one another's burdens, mourn with those that
mourn, comfort those in need of comfort, and witness for God
at all times, and in all places, and in all things (see Mosiah
18:8–9). Hubris, including intellectual pride, reflects the ways
of hell, not of heaven! No wonder a true community of scholars
would qualify to be part of a larger community of Saints.

The disciple-scholar also understands Jesus' style of leadership, which includes persuasion, long-suffering, gentleness,

meekness, love unfeigned, kindness, pure knowledge—all being achieved without hypocrisy and guile (see D&C 121:41–42; Mosiah 3:19). There again, wholeness and meekness are emphasized.

Consecrated Scholarship

The attribute of *knowledge* reflects more than the accumulation of assorted, uneven facts. It is "pure," and it is also not something apart; rather, it is closely associated with all other redeeming virtues. (See D&C 4:6; 107:30–31; 121:41–42; 2 Peter 1:5–9.)

Jesus is "the way, the truth, and the life" (John 14:6). Since He has received a fulness of truth, we rightly seek to have "the mind of Christ" (D&C 93:26; 1 Corinthians 2:16). If we keep His commandments, the promise is that we will receive "truth and light" until we are "glorified in truth and [know] all things" (D&C 93:28). Would either a true scholar or disciple settle for less?

In writing of C. S. Lewis, Paul L. Holmer wrote, "We can also say that in living right, we will also think right" (Paul L. Holmer, *C. S. Lewis, The Shape of His Faith and Thought* [New York: Harper and Row, 1976], p. 115).

Consecrated scholarship thus converges the life both of the mind and of the spirit!

Christ and the Creation

Restoration theology is expansive, not constraining. We do not face the problems Copernicus faced, when many mistakenly believed that the earth was the center of the universe.

For instance, through revelations we learn that Jesus played a remarkable role even premortally. Yet, given His stunning past, He was so meek! Under the direction of the Father, before His birth at Bethlehem, Jesus was actually the creating Lord of the universe. Clearly, God the Father is not the God of merely one planet!

Putting our planet in perspective Stephen W. Hawking wrote: "The earth is a medium-sized planet orbiting around an average star in the outer suburbs of an ordinary spiral galaxy, which is itself only one of about a million million galaxies in the observable universe" (*A Brief History of Time,* p. 126).

Figure 2 shows the placement of our comparatively tiny solar system in the suburbs of the Milky Way galaxy. The visuals will relate to the hymn we sang, "If You Could Hie to Kolob."

Figure 3 is the brightest portion of our "ordinary" Milky Way galaxy. This breathtaking view brings to mind the Lord's words about His having created "worlds without number" (Moses 1:33).

Figure 4 is a spiral galaxy—much like our galaxy, with millions of stars. This recalls the divine words that "there is no end to my works" (Moses 1:38).

Figure 5 is the Doradus Nebula. If it were as close to us as is very distant Orion, it would cover one-fourth of the night sky. Think of the words about how God's creations "cannot be numbered unto man, but they are numbered unto [Him]" (Moses 1:37).

Figure 6 is called Baade's Window. These myriad stars in just one region of the Milky Way galaxy recall the words "and the stars . . . give their light, as they roll upon their wings. . . . and any man who hath seen any or the least of these hath seen God moving in his majesty and power." (D&C 88:45, 47.)

When we contemplate the stunning vastness, it is wise to remember, "Behold . . . all things are created and made to bear record of me" (Moses 6:63). Alma similarly declared, "All things denote there is a God . . . all the planets which move in their regular form do witness that there is a Supreme Creator" (Alma 30:44). It is a witnessing and overwhelming universe!

At the other end of the spectrum of size we also see divine design in the tiny but significant DNA molecule. This molecule (figure 7), which performs so many large chores, is formed by a double, intertwined helix.

Figure 2

Figure 3

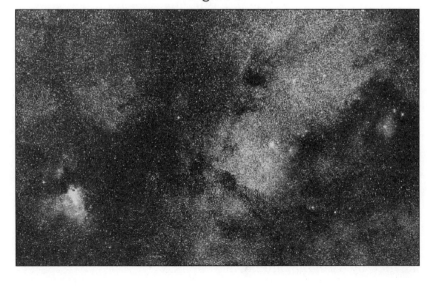

Figure 4

Figure 5

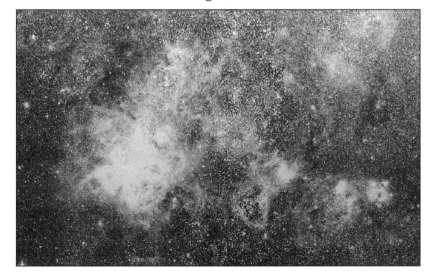

Figure 6

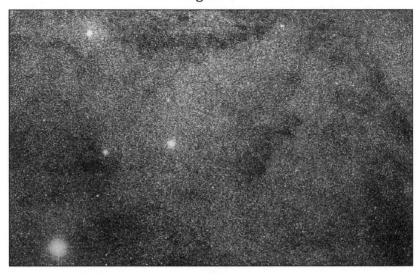

Figure 7

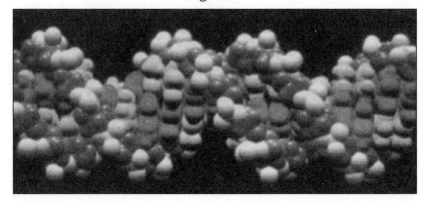

It is instructive that the Lord told Moses, "But only an account of this earth, and the inhabitants thereof, give I unto you" (Moses 1:35). Even so, the Lord has told us some soaring, salvational things: "That by [Christ], ... the worlds are and were created, and the inhabitants thereof are begotten sons and daughters unto God" (D&C 76:24).

Truly, "The heavens declare the glory of God; and the firmament sheweth his handywork" (Psalm 19:1), including the announcing star of Bethlehem.

Amid such cosmic *vastness* overseen by God and Jesus, however, we can also have faith in their loving *personal-ness*.

Does the Creator of the Universe Care About Us Individually?

We want to be assured that God is there, but also to know what is He like. We yearn to know what His and life's purposes are. Does He really know us and really care about us individually? The reassuring reality was confirmed in Enoch's exclamation: "And were it possible that man could number the particles of the earth, yea, millions of earths like this, it would not be a beginning to the number of thy creations; and thy curtains are stretched out still; and yet thou art there, and thy bosom is there; and also thou art just; thou art merciful and kind forever" (Moses 7:30).

The most important thing for meek Enoch to know was not how many worlds there were, but that God was really *there*! Moreover, Enoch also learned that God is *just, true,* and *merciful* (Moses 6:31; 7:30–31, 33, 37). We have an exemplifying Lord. Will we, however, follow His example?

When meek Enoch was first called by the Lord of the universe, he was unsure of himself: "And when Enoch had heard these words, he bowed himself to the earth, before the Lord, and spake before the Lord, saying: Why is it that I have found favor in thy sight, and am but a lad, and all the people hate me; for I am slow of speech; wherefore am I thy servant?" (Moses

6:31.) Yet much later meek Enoch had so deepened his discipleship that he actually came to know "that he pleased God" (Hebrews 11:5). Imagine the satisfaction of that knowledge!

Jesus gives such striking attention to individuals. To a woman from Samaria: "The woman saith unto him, I know that Messias cometh, which is called Christ: when he is come, he will tell us all things. Jesus saith unto her, I that speak unto thee am he." (John 4:25–26.) Jesus disclosed His true identity to an audience of one.

After His resurrection, Jesus, the Lord of the universe, visited Paul in a castle jail: "And the night following the Lord stood by him, and said, Be of good cheer, Paul; for as thou hast testified of me in Jerusalem, so must thou bear witness also at Rome" (Acts 23:11). Another audience of one!

It shouldn't surprise us that God gives so much individual attention to humans or to the divine design in the tiny DNA molecule. God "is in the details"—of the galaxies, of the DNA molecule, but, even more important, He "is in the details" of our lives.

Primary Attribute of the Disciple-Scholar: Meekness

There is as much vastness in the theology of the Restoration as in the stretching universe. "There is space there" for the full intellectual stretching of any serious disciple. There is room "enough and to spare" for all the behavioral development one is willing to undertake. No wonder, therefore, personal wholeness is required in discipleship. Genius without meekness is not enough to qualify for discipleship.

The portions of the key attributes lacking in each of us vary from person to person. It is meekness which facilitates working on what is lacking. For instance, the rich, righteous young man, otherwise clearly a high achiever, who came to Jesus asking what he might do to have eternal life, was told,

"One thing thou lackest" (Mark 10:21; see also Luke 18:22). His lack was not of marketplace acumen or of honesty in business affairs; instead, he lacked meekness. This, alas, kept him from doing that customized thing which Jesus asked him to do—sell all that he had, give to the poor, and come follow Him. The young man lacked consecration.

Oliver Cowdery, who devotedly helped the Restoration in so many other ways, couldn't translate as he had hoped. He apparently lacked intellectual diligence, thinking all he had to do was ask. Also he "did not continue as [he] commenced"; he also feared, and "the time is past" said the Lord. (D&C 9:5, 11.) How many times in life do opportunities pass us by for want of meekness, never to return?

Moses was meek enough but needed to make a major change in his leadership style—for both his and the people's sake. He was advised by Jethro to delegate—not only in order to be a more effective leader but also so he could better serve others by focusing on the things that mattered most in his ministry. "And thou shalt teach them ordinances and laws, and shalt shew them the way wherein they must walk, and the work that they must do." (See Exodus 18:17–22.)

Moses changed. No wonder he was referred to in the scriptures as "very meek, above all the men which were upon the face of the earth" (Numbers 12:3).

Peter was courageous and, understandably, thought he would never desert Jesus. Later, in an excruciating exchange, lack of full faith was underscored. This brought back Jesus' invitation to a humbled Peter—that when Peter was fully converted, he was to strengthen his brethren (Luke 22:32; see also John 21:15–17). So often the invitation to greater consecration comes by means of painful, personal experiences.

As Michael Polyani noted, "To learn by example is to submit to authority" (Michael Polyani, *Personal Knowledge: Towards a Post-Critical Philosophy* [Chicago: The University of Chicago Press, 1958], p. 53).

Ponder what Brigham Young said of his tutorial relationship with Joseph Smith: "An angel never watched [Joseph]

closer than I did, and that is what has given me the knowledge
I have today. I treasure it up, and ask the Father, in the name
of Jesus, to help my memory when information is wanted."
(Brigham Young Papers, 8 October 1866 sermon.)

May I shift for a few minutes to the secular scene. In the
opinion of Clement Attlee, Winston Churchill was England's
greatest wartime leader ever. Nevertheless, Churchill often
neglected and was insensitive to his wartime coalition cabinet
colleagues, including Attlee. At times Churchill put on a "one-
man show." In frustration, Attlee, Deputy Prime Minister, once
wrote a sharp letter to Churchill. ". . . I should have thought
that you would have reposed some confidence in your Cabinet
colleagues, but on the contrary you exhibit a very scanty
respect for their views." (Kenneth Harris, *Attlee* [London:
Weidenfeld and Nicolson, 1982], p. 242.) Attlee then spelled
out an irrefutable bill of particulars. Churchill was "thunder-
struck" and indignantly checked the feedback with his wife,
Lord Beaverbrook, and another friend—all of whom quickly
and candidly confirmed its accuracy.

Winston Churchill was wise in many respects, however.
He presciently chose as the motto for his last volume of World
War II history these words: "How the Great Democracies
Triumphed, and so Were Able to Resume the Follies Which
Had so Nearly Cost Them Their Life" (Winston S. Churchill,
The Second World War, vol. 6: *Triumph and Tragedy* [Boston:
Houghton Mifflin Company, 1953], p. ix).

One great individual who had considerable meekness was
George Washington. Of him, his biographer wrote: "In all history few men who possessed unassailable power have used
that power so gently and self-effacingly for what their best
instincts told them was the welfare of their neighbors and all
mankind" (James Thomas Flexner, *Washington, The Indispen-
sable Man* [New York: Plume, 1984], p. xvi).

Washington's was "the charisma of competence," wrote
Richard Norton Smith. Unlike Churchill, Washington was not
an orator, and he knew it, saying: "With me it has always been
a maxim rather to let my designs appear from my works than

by my expressions" (Richard Norton Smith, *Patriarch: George Washington and the New American Nation* [Boston: Houghton Mifflin Company, 1993], pp. 8, 12).

We are in a period in which so many are fascinated by charisma or seek for empowerment. Power to do what, however? This is the relevant question. Clever and evil, Hitler and Stalin (along with their combined henchmen) certainly had vast power. They helped to account for the premature losses of life in Greater Europe between 1930 and 1953 of an estimated 40–50 million people—as a result of wars and famine, massacres, purges, and exterminations. This man-made destructiveness is without precedent in human history! (See Alan Bullock, *Hitler and Stalin* [New York: Vintage Books, 1993], p. 969.)

What Fyodor Dostoevski wrote about power in "Notes from the House of the Dead" surely applies, and not alone to Hitler and Stalin: "Whoever has experienced the power, the complete ability to humiliate another human being . . . with the most extreme humiliation, willy-nilly loses power over his own sensations. Tyranny is a habit, it has a capacity for development, it develops finally into a disease. . . . Blood and power are intoxicating. . . . The human being and the citizen die within the tyrant forever; return to humanity, to repentance, to regeneration, becomes almost impossible." (In Bullock, *Hitler and Stalin,* pp. 971–72.)

Hitler had a certain charisma, all right, which Washington did not. But what about consequences?

Lincoln wrote of the incessant strivings for glory, especially among the talented: "It is to deny, what the history of the world tells us is true, to suppose that men of ambition and talents will not continue to spring up amongst us. . . . Towering genius disdains a beaten path. It seeks regions hitherto unexplored. It sees no distinction in adding story to story, upon the monuments of fame, erected to the memory of others. It denies that it is glory enough to serve under any chief. It scorns to tread in the footsteps of any predecessor, however illustrious. It thirsts and burns for distinction; and, if possible, it will have it, whether at the expense of emancipating slaves, or enslaving freemen." (Don E. Fehrenbacher, ed., *Abraham Lincoln: A Documentary Portrait Through His Speeches and Writings* [New York: The New American Library, 1964], p. 41.)

Power is safest, therefore, with those most Christlike, and heaven's power is accessible only to such individuals. No wonder the Lord warns us that power and authority, as used by the natural man, are abused by "almost all"! (See D&C 121:34–46.)

Thomas Merton noted Gandhi's searching question: "How can he who thinks he possesses absolute truth be fraternal?" (In Neal A. Maxwell, *A More Excellent Way* [Salt Lake City: Deseret Book, 1967], p. 31.) Obviously, the answer is for truth to company with love and meekness—as exemplified for us in the character of Jesus.

Do we have adequate faith in Jesus' character and in His atonement to strive genuinely to become more like Him, including in meekness?

The Great and Spacious Building

Do you remember the great and spacious building in the Book of Mormon? The trendy, self-congratulating multitudes were "politically correct" as they unmeekly mocked and pointed at those who clung to the gospel's iron rod. A few whose hands had once grasped the iron rod ended up in the great and spacious building pointing fingers of scorn at former friends. Strange as it seems, the scriptures do not indicate that these individuals let go of the iron rod for any objective reasons, or because they were in truth intellectually persuaded by the views of those in the great and spacious building. They were simply ashamed and embarrassed to be separated from the worldly multitudes, whose contempt they would not endure. "And after they had partaken of the fruit of the tree they did cast their eyes about as if they were ashamed" (1 Nephi 8:25).

No wonder Jesus, who "endured the cross, despising the

shame" (Hebrews 12:2), asks us to do likewise (see D&C 56:2). Jesus "gave no heed" to temptations either (D&C 20:22).

There is a certain security which comes of spiritual wholeness. Thomas More's words to his mortal judges reflected both his integrity and his generosity. Having been sentenced to die, he said to his judges: "Like the Blessed Apostle St. Paul, as we read in the Acts of the Apostles, was present, and consented to the death of St. Stephen, and kept their clothes that stoned him to death, and yet be they now both twain Holy Saints in heaven, and shall continue there friends forever, so I verily trust and shall therefore right heartily pray, that though your lordships have now here in earth been judges to my condemnation, we may yet hereafter in heaven merrily all meet together, to our everlasting salvation" (Anthony Kenny, *Thomas More* [New York: Oxford University Press, 1983], p. 88).

More gave no heed to the contempt in which he was held by his accusers, but was not contemptuous of them.

The Path to Discipleship

The sooner we are on the way to serious discipleship, therefore, the sooner the needed spiritual and personal reinforcements and intellectual reassurances will come to us personally. If one chooses to live out his life without God, however, it will be as if he had been sentenced to remain a permanent resident in an airport transit lounge—consigned there, briefly and expectantly, to mingle with the ever-changing, lonely crowds. Somehow, in that forlorn situation, even being granted a cot and a hotplate in the corner of the transit lounge would not ease either the sense of anomie or futility.

Someday, in the search for wholeness in thought and behavior, we shall see much more clearly how orthodoxy "is our reward, not solely our goad" (Paul L. Holmer, *C. S. Lewis, The Shape of His Faith and Thought,* p. 115).

Genius is safest when it is accompanied by meekness.

Competency is most useful when accompanied by humility. The qualities of love, mercy, patience, meekness, and spiritual submissiveness are portable. These—to the degree developed—will go with us through the veil of death; they will also rise with us in the resurrection.

No matter how many talents or gifts we now have, God will still seek to remodel us, if we will let Him. Borrowing a parable from George MacDonald, C. S. Lewis wrote of such painful remodeling:

> Imagine yourself as a living house. God comes in to rebuild that house. At first, perhaps, you can understand what He is doing. He is getting the drains right and stopping the leaks in the roof and so on: you knew that those jobs needed doing and so you are not surprised. But presently he starts knocking the house about in a way that hurts abominably and does not seem to make sense. What on earth is He up to? The explanation is that He is building quite a different house from the one you thought of—throwing out a new wing here, putting on an extra floor there, running up towers, making courtyards. You thought you were going to be made into a decent little cottage: but He is building a palace. (C. S. Lewis, *Mere Christianity* [New York: Macmillan, 1952], p. 174.)

Long before being a General Authority, I remarked on how in the world some academic men and women are blind in one eye. These are quick to see dangers coming from the one direction, but not from other directions. Only the eyes of faith permit us to see "things as they really are, and . . . things as they really will be" (Jacob 4:13). The disciple-scholar is concerned with knowing and responding to such reality. He also values history. But history, by itself, has its limitations, as Churchill observed:

> History with its flickering lamps stumbles along the trail of the past, trying to reconstruct its scenes, to revive its echoes, and kindle with pale gleams the passion of former days. . . . The only guide to a man is his conscience; the only shield to his

memory is the rectitude and sincerity of his actions. It is very imprudent to walk through life without this shield, because we are so often mocked by the failure of our hopes and the upsetting of our calculations; but with this shield, however the fates may play, we march always in the ranks of honor. (In Robert Rhodes James, ed., *Churchill Speaks* [W. H. Smith and Son, USA, Winward Press, 1981], p. 734.)

The Holy Ghost, which gift the disciple has, provides precious proportion. Otherwise, as Owen Barfield wrote, there occurs a "whisper" which "Memory will warehouse as a shout" (Wayne Martindale and Jerry Root, eds., *The Quotable C. S. Lewis* [Wheaton, Illinois; Tyndale House Publishers, 1989], p. 424.)

To be a disciple-scholar in our time is a call to high adventure! Just as one's quest for knowledge should be unending, so too should the quest for greater love, meekness, and patience.

Consecration and the Disciple-Scholar

In considering consecration, it is well to remember that under this principle nothing is held back—whether turf, attitude, or hobbies. One's will is to be swallowed up in the will of God—just as occurred with Jesus (see Mosiah 15:7).

Though I have spoken of the disciple-scholar, in the end all the hyphenated words come off. We are finally disciples—men and women of Christ (see 3 Nephi 27:27).

But is consecration asking too much? It is certainly asking more than but a few finally achieve. It certainly involves a submission to authority, but what an Authority!

When we consecrate, individuality is actually enhanced, not lost. Our quirks and impurities go, but who would want to come into the Inner Court trailing such obsolete trinkets anyway? Besides, it is easier to be a character than to have character!

Why is it all so slow? Because God will not impose upon us.

In opting for discipleship, we have nothing to fear but the disapproval of the natural man and his like-minded, preoccupied friends—with their pointing fingers.

Most forms of holding back are rooted in pride or are prompted by the mistaken notion that somehow we are diminished by submission to God. Actually, the greater the submission, the greater the expansion!

Where will the journey take us? "Unto a perfect man, unto the measure of the stature of the fulness of Christ" (Ephesians 4:13). One who "continueth in God, receiveth more light; and that light groweth brighter and brighter until the perfect day" (D&C 50:24). There isn't any shortcut. The straight and narrow is the quickest and most direct way. It is also the only way!

Will there be perplexities? Yes, indeed. "I know that [God] loveth his children; nevertheless, I do not know the meaning of all things" (1 Nephi 11:17). Indeed, we too will not always know the "meaning" of things happening to us and around us. Therefore, whatever knowledge we may have, we still need to have faith to see us through those puzzling moments. Because of past verifying experiences, we can know that we have proven God "in days that are past," thus giving us faith for the challenges of the present.

God bless you who are in the vanguard of special spirits in these the last days, in the name of Jesus Christ, amen.

2

PAUL ALAN COX

Journey to City Creek: Adding Scholarship to Discipleship

The first goal of the Honors Program at BYU is to model the compatibility of rigorous scholarship with deep commitment to the faith, including institutional aspects of that faith. The development of discipleship in young scholars has been beautifully discussed by Elder Maxwell in the inaugural Discipline and Discipleship lecture. His themes of developing the attitudes of meekness, submissiveness, and consecration in the disciple-scholar will be explored in subsequent lectures. Tonight at this annual Honors Banquet I would like to consider an alternative issue: the development of scholarship in young disciples. Why should young disciples of Jesus Christ pursue an education? Can an education equip young disciples for more than earning a living—can education assist young disciples in better serving the kingdom of God?

Should Disciples Seek Learning?

The word *scholar* comes from the Latin word *scholaris,* which translates as "pertaining to a school." Although *scholar* is commonly used to signify a learned person, the dictionary indicates it also means "a student; a person attending school." It is this second and older definition that I would like to use. Specifically, I would like to address not only BYU Honors students but also all Latter-day Saint students wherever they may be, including many who see themselves as struggling. In using this older definition of *scholar,* I include many young people who may not identify themselves with the words *scholarly* or *scholarship,* those who may not consider themselves capable of securing admission into selective universities or programs, and particularly those who are wondering if they really should continue to pursue an education. I want to tell you why I personally believe that, despite all odds, you should seek learning.

The Church of Jesus Christ, from the time of the Savior even until now, has been largely composed of working people, individuals who pursue honorable professions and trades common to the societies in which they live. Jesus commented on the diversity of people who would be gathered into the kingdom: "Again, the kingdom of heaven is like unto a net, that was cast into the sea, and gathered of every kind" (Matthew 13:47). Unlike some other religions, the gospel of Jesus Christ does not grant special status to theologians, philosophers, or other academics. All are welcome to enjoy the bounteous blessings of the gospel, regardless of educational background or social status (see 2 Nephi 26:24–28). Those called by the Savior to serve in His kingdom represent this broad cross-section of humanity. Jesus Christ, raised by Mary and by Joseph the carpenter, first called as His disciples fishermen and others engaged in common professions. Paul noted this fact in his letter to the Corinthians: "For ye see your calling, brethren, how that not many wise men after the flesh, not many mighty, not many noble, are called: but God hath chosen the foolish things of the world to confound the wise; and God hath chosen the weak things of the world to confound the things which are mighty" (1 Corinthians 1:26–27).

Academic credentials are not requisite for service in the Lord's kingdom. Indeed there are explicit warnings within the scriptures to both the rich and the learned to avoid pride. Yet we can see within such scriptures an intriguing pattern: the warnings to the learned are often given by prophets and Apostles who have themselves sought learning. Paul, for example, was a student of Gamaliel and an associate of the Sanhedrin. He gained fluency in several languages, and, as demonstrated by his masterful address on Mars Hill, was conversant with Greek philosophy. Given his own educational attainments, is it safe to construe Paul's statement that God hath "made foolish the wisdom of this world" (1 Corinthians 1:20) as an injunction for Christ's disciples to remain unlearned?

Examples of learned prophets cautioning the learned against pride can also be found in the Book of Mormon. Consider the familiar warning of Jacob's: "O the vainness, and the frailties, and the foolishness of men! When they are learned they think they are wise, and they hearken not unto the counsel of God, for they set it aside, supposing they know of themselves, wherefore, their wisdom is foolishness and it profiteth them not. And they shall perish." (2 Nephi 9:28.)

Some may take this warning to mean that disciples should avoid learning at all costs. Yet Jacob's brother and exemplar, the prophet Nephi, in the very first sentence in the Book of Mormon unabashedly tells us of his own obtaining an education: "I, Nephi, having been born of goodly parents, therefore I was taught somewhat in all the learning of my father" (1 Nephi 1:1). However, even though Nephi had intensively studied Egyptian and Hebrew, he later chastised "the wise, and the learned . . . that are puffed up in the pride of their hearts" (2 Nephi 28:15). This pattern of learned prophets rebuking the prideful learned was also exemplified by Abinadi, who confounded the wicked priests of King Noah by reciting from memory the complete text of Isaiah 53 (see Mosiah 14), knowledge that he likely gained from his own intensive study of the scriptures. The pattern also occurs with Mormon, who tells us that as a child he sought education after the manner of his people, and was "sober" and "quick to observe" (Mormon 1:2). Mormon's son Moroni apparently saw himself as a struggling student, fearing that his latter-day readers might condemn him because of "his imperfection" (Mormon 9:31) and "weakness in writing" (Ether 12:23). Yet he discussed with considerable aplomb the relative merits of inscribing plates in Hebrew and reformed Egyptian, revealing a knowledge of both languages as well as his native tongue (Moroni 9:31).

Even Joseph Smith, who referred to himself as "an unlearned boy" (*Teachings of the Prophet Joseph Smith,* p. 371), was able not only to recognize excerpts from Malachi 4, Isaiah 11, Acts 3, and Joel 2 when quoted to him by the angel Moroni, but also noticed subtle changes in these texts during Moroni's recitation (see Joseph Smith—History 1:36–41). Clearly many of the Lord's servants, both former and current, struggled to obtain an education through whatever means was available to them. Should we not then consider Jacob's assertion that "to be learned is good if they hearken unto the counsels of God" (2 Nephi 9:29) as an encouragement for those who seek discipleship to also actively pursue learning, rather than as a warning against education?

My Personal Question: Should I Study Botany?

The answer to the question "Should I study botany?" was not apparent to me as a young student attempting to determine my future career. I had a firm testimony of the restoration of the gospel and wanted to pursue a career useful to the kingdom. My father was a park ranger. He built beautiful trails and parks. My grandfather built fish hatcheries and wildlife refuges. The fruits of their labors are very tangible and continue to bless the lives of thousands. Although I loved plants and wanted to study botany, I wondered if I shouldn't follow the path of my father and grandfather and become a park ranger. What good would studying plants do for the world? Wouldn't it be better to avoid esoteric studies and seek training in practical pursuits?

Although the members of the Church early in this dispensation established schools and sought higher education, their skills in farming, blacksmithing, bricklaying, and other honorable trades facilitated the colonization of the Great Basin. Given this emphasis on practical skills, are there ways that scholarship can add to discipleship? Is there a role for scholars in the kingdom of God? Let me share with you a recent journey that gave me some insight into this question, my personal journey to City Creek.

City Creek and the Arrival of the Saints in Utah

On 6 April 1993 I sat alone in a rented cabin attempting to finish a manuscript about my search for new medicinal drugs from rain forest plants. The morning light was bright on the snow, but I was oblivious to my surroundings. My fingers danced over the keyboard as I typed my last paragraph. I was elated. My scientific paper was finished, yet it was only 10:30 A.M. There was time for me to put my plan into action. I changed into a suit, jumped into my vehicle, and headed toward Salt Lake City. I had decided to make a journey to City Creek.

City Creek was first sighted by the pioneers on the afternoon of 22 July 1847 when they arrived in the valley of the Great Salt Lake. They set up camp on its south fork. I have spent a bit of time attempting to locate the precise site of that camp. In those days City Creek immediately divided as it entered the valley (Draper 1988). The west branch cut through a corner of the future temple block beneath where the statue of Christus currently stands in the Temple Square visitors center. It then turned immediately west. The south branch ran where the Main Street of Salt Lake City now is, and then branched again. One branch ran northwest while the other continued south down the current course of Main Street, turning west near Fourth South. As far as I can determine, the campsite of those first pioneers is buried beneath Main Street somewhere near the current site of the Crossroads Mall shopping center.

In 1847 the scene along City Creek was barren: there were only two or three cottonwood trees, and the ground was dry and hard. The pioneers immediately tried to plant potatoes, but several plows were broken in the attempt. To soften the ground, a small dam was built. When Brigham Young saw the dam a few days later, he "regretted the destruction of the willows and wild roses growing on the banks of City Creek" (Roberts, 235). On 28 July Brigham Young walked upstream with a small party to a point between the two upper branches. He struck his cane on the ground and declared, "Here we shall build a temple to our God." Tradition has it that Wilford Woodruff then drove a stake into the ground to mark the spot (Holzapfel, p. 5).

Work on the Salt Lake Temple Commences

Due to the stark demands for survival, the early pioneers could not begin work on the temple for six years. But on Valentine's Day, 14 February 1853, the Saints gathered to the temple site for the groundbreaking. The cold and snow made this a very different sort of occasion than the pleasant ceremonies we associate with current groundbreakings. The poverty of the Saints was appalling. One member of the Church recorded: "I walked [to the meeting] the morning the ground was broken for the foundation of the Temple . . . on the Temple Block. I went through frozen mud and slush with my feet tied up in rags. I had on a pair of pants made out of my wife's skirt—a thin Scotch plaid; also a thin calico shirt and a straw hat. These were all the clothes I had. . . . I was not alone in poverty. . . . There were many who were fixed as badly as I was." (Holzapfel, p. 9.)

The ground itself was frozen and covered by three inches of snow. Wilford Woodruff wrote: "The ground being frozen, President Heber C. Kimball commenced breaking the ground with a pick. . . . Then the ground was broke and President Young took out the first turf." (Holzapfel, p. 10.)

The next week President Young assigned Elder Woodruff to assist in digging out the foundation in preparation for laying the cornerstones. Wilford Woodruff worked hard at this taxing labor. Normally a prodigious diary writer, during one week he made only a single entry in his journal: "March 14, 15, 16, 17, 18, and 19th I spent this week in digging out the foundation for the Temple" (Holzapfel, p. 10).

The value of learning in preparation for service to the kingdom is apparent from the design Brigham Young prepared for the Salt Lake Temple. As a youth, Brigham Young had apprenticed as a cabinetmaker and later studied glazing and carpentry. The economic circumstances of his family made further education impossible, but Brigham Young's 1840–41 mission provided an opportunity for him to be exposed to the great historical and architectural monuments of England. He was fascinated by St. Paul's Cathedral, the Tower of London, and Westminster Abbey, for which he purchased a detailed architectural guide. He also visited Worcester Cathedral with Wilford Woodruff. His self-directed study of British architecture helped prepare President Young to design, through inspiration, the general appearance of the Salt Lake Temple. The importance of his mission study of English cathedrals and monuments was apparent in the way he called the temple architect, Truman Angell, on a mission to England in 1856 to study architecture, prior to drafting detailed plans for the Salt Lake Temple. In his blessing to Brother Angell, Brigham Young promised: "You shall have power and means to go from place to place, from country to country, and view the various specimens of architecture that you may desire to see, and you will wonder at the works of the ancients and marvel to see what they have done" (Hamilton and Cutrubus, p. 52).

Just as City Creek had nourished the early pioneers, it now began to nourish the work of the temple construction. Brigham Young's inspiration in locating the temple adjacent to City Creek became clear when a waterwheel, sixteen feet in diameter, was placed in City Creek to turn the lathes for the temple carpentry shops. That waterwheel also drove an air flume for the blacksmith shop (Raynor, p. 26). Tradition has it that City Creek also powered one of the early versions of the Tabernacle organ.

City Creek changed as Salt Lake City grew. It was only with tremendous difficulty that the massive granite stairways, with each step weighing 1,700 pounds, could be incorporated in the emerging temple. Yet in 1878, steam engines, with water supplied from City Creek, replaced manpower and horsepower in pulling the massive granite blocks, some in excess of 5,600 pounds, to the top of the temple walls. (Raynor, pp. 110–26.)

Dedication of the Salt Lake Temple

Thirty-nine years of sacrifice and backbreaking toil led to the laying of the capstone on 6 April 1892. Salt Lake City was packed: some fifty thousand people, twice the capacity of BYU's Marriott Center, jammed Temple Square and packed into the surrounding streets. Some sat on the tops of houses, and a few even climbed telegraph poles to see the ceremony.

President Wilford Woodruff, who had personally participated in digging the foundation so many years before, now raised both hands above his head and announced to the crowd: "Attention all ye house of Israel, and all ye nations of the earth! We will now lay the top-stone of the Temple of our God, the foundation of which was laid and dedicated by the Prophet, Seer, and Revelator, Brigham Young." He pushed a button, and the capstone settled into place.

President Lorenzo Snow then led the Saints in the Hosanna Shout. Imagine fifty thousand people, with tears streaming down their faces, all crying aloud three times: "Hosanna! Hosanna! Hosanna! to God and the Lamb! Amen! Amen! Amen!"

"The scene . . . [was] beyond the power of language to describe," a Church member visiting from Idaho wrote. "The eyes of thousands were moistened with tears in the fullness of their joy. The ground seemed to tremble with the volume of the sound which sent forth its echoes to the surrounding hills." (Holzapfel, p. 46.)

The capstone was laid. The walls were built, but there remained far more to do: the interior had to be completed. A motion was made to the multitude to complete the interior of the temple in one year's time. A "deafening" roar of "ayes" was returned from the thousands present. Every Saint pledged his or her utmost to the goal. James E. Talmage first pledged an amount equal (and in addition to) his full tithing; then later, in response to a further appeal, he increased the amount by two-thirds. Craftsmen and artisans of every type, including returning art missionaries from Europe, hastened to complete the work in the allotted time. This temple was finished during a period of deep economic recession. The people were poor. But they gave everything they could in time, talents, and funds to the construction of that temple.

Their haste to complete the temple did not mean that they produced shoddy workmanship. They believed that only the best was acceptable to the Lord. Through prayer, fasting, and a tremendous amount of hard manual labor they succeeded in completing the temple interior only the night before the dedication.

A Ticket to the Original Temple Dedication

As I drove from my cabin toward City Creek on 6 April 1993, I owned an original ticket to the dedication of the Salt

Lake Temple. The ticket belonged to my grandmother, who as a young girl had attended the temple dedication, and it was given to me by my mother before she died.

Arriving in Salt Lake, I called at the nearby office of a close friend who is a prominent bond attorney. Together we walked down the little artificial stream behind the Church Administration building that runs, much like City Creek before it, toward the temple site. I wanted to worship in the Salt Lake Temple a hundred years to the day from its original dedication.

When we entered the temple I was stunned by the intensity of the Spirit present. Even though the building was packed with people, the Spirit was beautiful and serene. We changed into white clothing and walked into the small chapel. Instead of sitting with the rest of the patrons we sat alone in an unoccupied area. After fifteen minutes a member of the temple presidency announced that the temple was so full that day that not all of us could be admitted for ordinance work. Those seated on the other side of the chapel were invited to attend the endowment session. Although I was not chosen, I was still happy because the Spirit of the Lord filled the temple. I would have been pleased just to sit in the chapel or even in the locker room all afternoon.

And then something extraordinary happened. A counselor in the temple presidency spoke to us and the few other remaining patrons: "I'm sorry we can't accommodate you today in a session. I have never done this before, but this is an extraordinary day. How would you like a tour of the temple?"

Superb Workmanship in the Solemn Assembly Room

We silently ascended the northwest staircase. As we walked, I thought of each granite step, 1,700 pounds in weight, being carved and then hoisted by hand into place. There was a hush as we entered the Solemn Assembly room on the fourth floor.

The room was beautiful. I felt as though I had entered heaven. In each corner stands a beautiful freestanding staircase. The handiwork is exquisite, with small stars carved into the wood even beneath the staircase. Light streams through the large oval windows. Each brass doorknob bears a beehive and the words "Holiness to the Lord." The carving, the painting, the architecture, and the grandeur of the room are overwhelming.

"Where was the actual dedication ceremony held?" I asked the temple president. "My grandmother attended when she was a child."

"Right here where you are sitting—right here in the Solemn Assembly room."

I thought of the labor and the sacrifice and the love that had gone into building the temple. And while I thought about it I was deeply humbled. "I'm not a craftsman," I thought." I can't carve stone. I can't paint. I can't upholster. I can't create beautiful handiwork in wood. What place do I have in the house of the Lord? What could I have possibly contributed to this effort?"

This is hard for me to articulate, but remember that my progenitors were working people who created tangible results with their labor. To contemplate such beauty and sacrifice and grandeur and to realize that I would have had nothing to contribute to such a glorious enterprise was deeply sobering. "What can I contribute?" I prayed silently. "What is there that I as a botanist have to offer the kingdom?"

The counselor invited us to accompany him out of the Solemn Assembly room and through a narrow hallway. We entered a small office. In it sat a small rolltop desk. "This is where James E. Talmage wrote *Jesus the Christ,*" our guide explained.

As I stared at that desk, I suddenly realized that there is a place for scholars in the Lord's house. Our craft is not better than stonecutting or woodworking or painting, but neither is it inferior. All have their place. All have a contribution to make in the kingdom. If we approach the lofty goal of becoming disciple-scholars, as Elder Maxwell discussed in his lecture, our scholarly contributions can become as consecrated as the stone from the temple quarry.

Is there a place for botany in the kingdom? Is there a place for econometrics, and medieval studies, and chemistry, and ancient languages, and all of the other disciplines that we study here? Can acquisition of higher education help disciples contribute to the building of the kingdom? I'm convinced that it can, but only if we adopt the qualities Elder Maxwell so clearly set before us in the first Discipline and Discipleship lecture. Quoting Mosiah 3:19, he told us that we should "[become] as a child, submissive, meek, humble, patient, full of love, willing to submit to all things which the Lord seeth fit to inflict upon [us]."

Are there any individuals who model this high standard? The rush of spiritual insight as I looked at that little rolltop desk in the temple that day inspired me further to examine the life and personality of Elder James E. Talmage. As I returned to BYU, I called a friend in the BYU library to see if we had a copy of Elder Talmage's journals. "We not only have a copy, Paul, we have the originals," he replied. "Come over and we'll let you see them."

James E. Talmage as a Disciple-Scholar

Elder Talmage was a superb geologist who published in the leading scientific journals of his day. Yet he modeled in his life the qualities of meekness, humility, and submission to priesthood authority that Elder Maxwell indicated as characteristic of the disciple-scholar. These spiritual characteristics helped prepare him for his call into the Quorum of the Twelve in December 1911. During his ordination to the holy apostleship Elder Talmage was blessed by President Joseph F. Smith to "have the spirit of humility and meekness even more abundantly than you have ever experienced it heretofore." This humble spirit, combined with his lifelong quest for learning, helped prepare him to write one of the greatest Church books of this dispensation: *Jesus the Christ.* Let me share with you a few excerpts from Elder Talmage's journals, written during the period when he was writing that book.

On 14 September 1914, Elder Talmage wrote: "I delivered a series of lectures entitled 'Jesus the Christ,' under the auspices of the University Sunday School. . . . I have received written appointment from the First Presidency to embody the lectures in a book for the use of the Church in general. Experiences demonstrated that neither in my comfortable office nor in the convenient study room at home can I be free from visits and telephone calls . . . , and in view of the importance of the work, I have been directed to occupy a room in the Temple where I will be free from interruption."

He devoted all free moments of his time to writing, and even had a little cot placed in his temple room. Like a true scholar, he burnt the midnight oil. "Since I began my work on the Life of Christ," he wrote on 30 September, "I have devoted every possible hour to the lesson, oft-times working in the Temple until a late hour at night."

Elder Talmage worked at the manuscript on Thanksgiving Day, most of Christmas Day, New Year's Day and every holiday. Finally he wrote in his journal on 19 April: "Finished the actual writing on the book 'Jesus the Christ,' to which I have devoted every spare hour since settling down to the work of composition on September 14th last. Had it not been that I was privileged to do this work in the Temple, it would be at present far from completion. I have felt the inspiration of the place and have appreciated the privacy and quietness incident thereto."

But Elder Talmage did not immediately publish his masterpiece. He read it chapter by chapter to the First Presidency and Twelve Apostles, seeking their criticism and approval. As recorded in his diary, between 17 April and 24 June 1915 he met eighteen times with these priesthood leaders, and read them every single word of his book. Only then did he pass the manuscript to the printer.

In the light of Elder Talmage's example, consider again Jacob's warning and his promise to the learned: "O the vainness, and the frailties, and the foolishness of men! When they are learned they think they are wise, and they hearken not unto the counsel of God, for they set it aside, supposing they know of themselves, wherefore, their wisdom is foolishness and it profiteth them not. And they shall perish. But to be learned is good if they hearken unto the counsels of God." (2 Nephi 9:28–29.)

One of the meanings of the word *counsel* is "opinion or instruction given for directing the judgment or conduct of another; opinion or direction given upon request." Although he had written a masterpiece, Elder James E. Talmage meekly sought the counsel of the Lord's servants by reading every single word of his manuscript of *Jesus the Christ* to the presiding councils of the Church before the work was published. Jacob was right: "To be learned is good," if a disciple hearkens "to the counsels of God." Elder Talmage was learned, but he hearkened to the counsels of God. His actions demonstrated meekness, humility, and submissiveness to priesthood authority, the key attributes of a disciple-scholar identified by Elder Maxwell.

Adding Scholarship to Discipleship

Few disciples will be called to produce written works as significant as *Jesus the Christ*. But in the temple that day I realized that learning can help me, too, make a contribution, however small, to the kingdom. I realized that the Salt Lake Temple was not built by a single individual, by a Brigham Young or a Wilford Woodruff. They played important roles, but ultimately the temple was built by the sacrifice of many thousands of individuals: those who sewed cloth and those who sowed crops, those who cut checks and those who cut stone. We don't know their names, but Heavenly Father does! Their selfless contributions continue to bless us today.

In a similar way, disciples who seek learning can help contribute to the kingdom. Why should disciples seek learning? The answer is clearly given by the Lord in latter-day revelation:

> Teach ye diligently and my grace shall attend you, that you may be instructed more perfectly in theory, in principle, in doctrine, in the law of the gospel, in all things that pertain unto the kingdom of God, that are expedient for you to understand;
>
> Of things both in heaven and in the earth, and under the earth; things which have been, things which are, things which must shortly come to pass; things which are at home, things which are abroad; the wars and the perplexities of the nations, and the judgments which are on the land; and a knowledge also of countries and of kingdoms—
>
> That ye may be prepared in all things when I shall send you again to magnify the calling whereunto I have called you, and the mission with which I have commissioned you (D&C 88:78–80).

Learning is important for disciples because it helps qualify them "to magnify the calling whereunto I have called you." In the case of Brigham Young, that calling included determining the general appearance of the Salt Lake Temple. In the case of James Talmage, that calling included writing *Jesus the Christ*. For all of us, obeying the Lord's command to "seek learning, even by study and also by faith" (D&C 88:118; 109:7) will help us increase our ability to serve the Church in many different ways.

Acquisition of learning can also help a craftsman to become a better craftsman. Joseph Bennion and his wife, Lee, began a pottery and art business in Spring City, a small Utah town. In the beginning Joseph made pots for the mass market, selling them mainly at crafts fairs. But although he was a good potter, he felt compelled to return to school. There his study of Native American cultures and values began to influence his philosophy about art. In a university setting he also was forced to defend pottery as a viable art form rather than merely as a craft. As a result his craftsmanship deepened. He began to shift his sights from the mass market and started making pots that have deep spiritual and aesthetic values. Today, though his work is produced primarily for a local market, Joseph Bennion is nationally recognized. His ceramics command increasing attention in serious art exhibitions. A film on his work that emphasizes the wholesome, gospel orientation of his family has won national acclaim.

Another young Latter-day Saint, Kurt Bestor, composes musical scores for the film industry. His father told me that Kurt's tremendous gift for music was obvious even when Kurt was a child. Although Kurt could have begun his profession without further studies, he sought a college degree. Kurt explains that the discipline of a college education honed his craft even further. "Now when I have a client tell me they want something that sounds like Mozart's *Requiem,* I know what they mean because I studied the score in college. Right now I'm composing some Dixieland music, an idiom I know because I played in a Dixieland band while in school."

On occasion Kurt has been called by the Church to compose music for films that are screened in the seminary program and in other sacred places. Kurt explains what happened during a priesthood blessing: "I realized that I came to earth to help create the best-quality music for the kingdom. If I hadn't pursued an education, the inefficiencies would have gotten in the way of my conveying the Spirit. If I hadn't pursued an education, when called I would have had to say 'I'm sorry, but I'm not ready.'"

Kurt believes that his children have been blessed because of his degree and the degree in humanities that his wife, Melodie, received. "When we talk to our children about literature, art, or music, they understand. Our education has helped us better to prepare our children, which is perhaps the greatest service anyone can render to the kingdom."

Another example of an entire family being blessed by learning is provided by my friends Kevin and Melody Clyde. Although Kevin became a manager in his family's road construction business at a young age, he continued to seek a degree in English literature. Often Kevin would read Long-fellow, Wordsworth, and even a little Latin poetry at night in a construction trailer near his work site. His wife, Melody, received a degree in art. Their children have been taught from an early age to value both literature and the arts and can talk knowledgeably about the major events in world history. Because of his skills in both literature and construction management, Kevin was recently offered the opportunity to begin a new career as headmaster of a private school.

City Creek as a Model of Giving

When I think about the examples of Joseph and Lee Bennion, Kurt and Melodie Bestor, and Kevin and Melody Clyde, I reflect on Brigham Young's statement on education: "Will education feed and clothe you, keep you warm on a cold day, or enable you to build a house? Not at all. Should we cry down education on this account? No. What is it for? The improvement of the mind; to instruct us in all arts and sciences, in the history of the world, in the laws of nations; to enable us to understand the laws and principles of life, and how to be useful while we live." (*Journal of Discourses* 14:83.)

Enabling us to "understand . . . how to be useful while we live" is perhaps the greatest reason for disciples to seek learning. Simply stated, adding scholarship to discipleship better prepares us to build the kingdom. Because of my little journey to City Creek, I know now that learned disciples can contribute to Zion just as surely as trained stonecutters contributed to building the Salt Lake Temple. Most such service will be quiet and largely anonymous, and when performed by "hearkening to the counsels of God" will indeed prove acceptable to Him.

Perhaps in that light we should seek to model our service after that provided by City Creek. No one seems to know much about City Creek today. It was only with some difficulty that I was able to discover its former course. But what an important role that stream played in building the kingdom!

City Creek quietly quenched the thirst of the pioneers, watered their crops, powered the waterwheel, provided the compression for the steam engine, gave breath to the Tabernacle organ, and in so many other ways performed a sacred and consecrated service. When I think of this relatively anonymous service of City Creek, I remember the words of the poet Theodore Roethke in his poem "The Longing."

> I would be a stream, winding between
> great striated rocks in late summer . . .
> Where shadow can change into flame
> And the dark be forgotten.

Truly along City Creek, where the Lord's house stands, the shadow has turned into flame, and dark has been forgotten. To those of you who are students, who struggle at night to learn from textbooks, who attend classes and lectures—often at great personal sacrifice—in the quest for learning, I assure you that your efforts will indeed be rewarded by an increased ability to serve. City Creek has become to me not only a journey but also a model, a model of giving I learned about long ago in my Primary classes:

> "Give," said the little stream,
> "Give, oh! give, give, oh! give."
> "Give," said the little stream,
> As it hurried down the hill;
> "I'm small, I know, but wherever I go,
> The fields grow greener still."
> (Fanny J. Crosby, "'Give,' said the Little
> Stream," in *Children's Songbook,* p. 236.)

I testify that if we become disciple-scholars as outlined by Elder Maxwell, we, like City Creek, can indeed contribute to the kingdom. That we may achieve this lofty goal is my prayer, in the name of Jesus Christ, amen.

Sources Cited

Draper, L. W. 1988. M.A. Thesis. Brigham Young University.
Hamilton, C. M., and Cutrubus, C. N. 1983. *The Salt Lake Temple: A Monument to a People.* University Services Corp., Salt Lake City.
Holzapfel, R. N. 1992. *Every Stone a Sermon.* Bookcraft, Salt Lake City.
Raynor, W. A. 1965. *The Everlasting Spires.* Deseret Book, Salt Lake City.
Roberts, B. H. 1930. *A Comprehensive History of the Church,* vol. 3. The Church of Jesus Christ of Latter-day Saints, Salt Lake City.

3

ELDER CECIL O. SAMUELSON, JR.

The Importance of Meekness in the Disciple-Scholar

I am honored to be invited by Dean Paul Cox to be with you tonight. I am aware of the quality of your Honors Program and the responsibility this generous invitation brings to me. Dean Cox suggested that I might focus my comments on the importance of meekness for the disciple-scholar. While I'm grateful that I am now old enough to be able to appreciate the importance of meekness in both discipleship and scholarship, I must confess that I am still at an awkward age in that I have yet to become appropriately meek in my own endeavors in either sphere. Nevertheless, with full appreciation that this assignment is really more for my growth than yours, I cheerfully accept the challenges to try to make some sense of this topic in our time together and also make meekness a much more reflexive behavior in my own life.

I have had the privilege of reviewing Elder Neal A. Maxwell's masterful treatise on the disciple-scholar which he shared with you in this lecture series last month. No direct comments from me about it would be appropriate or helpful to you, but it has been of great benefit to me personally. I love and sustain him for being a "master of meekness" in addition to all that his high and holy office elicits from one trying to be faithful in the kingdom. As a master teacher, he catalyzes scholarship in his students that might not occur otherwise, and I suspect that most of you have been beneficially stretched by his ideas as have I.

Even in this special setting at BYU that joins the values of disciples and scholars, I am concerned that there may be a temptation to unbalance the scales toward secular scholarship rather than toward spiritual stewardship. Therefore my focus tonight may be more to the sacred than to the scientific. This may not be your preference and it may provide more insight into my own deficiencies than into yours, should you have them.

Genius Without Meekness

Elder Maxwell has reminded us that "genius without meekness is nothing." Most of us have notions of what constitutes genius, and many of you, by definition of your inborn talents and their effective development, personally experience genius in at least parts of your own lives. These characteristics, or at least your potential to have them, probably played the major role in your admission to the Honors Program. The scriptures teach us, however, that the most important and certainly lasting honors (eternal life) are those much better described by traits such as meekness. Since this is clearly so, should not we then strive to become not only excellent scholars but also practitioners of meekness and companion virtues?

Webster defines *meekness* as a noun meaning patience and

long-suffering. Associated ideas include the capacity to bear pain or trials without complaint; self-control, calmness, tolerance, endurance of offenses, and so forth. The Topical Guide and Index in recent editions of the LDS scriptures link meekness with words like *contrite, gentle, humble, lowliness, poor, forbearance,* and *love.* It should be noted that a common syntactical usage that may denote a deficiency in spirit or courage has no place in our meaning or discussion. Likewise, we should not be confused by supposing that by meek we mean timid, tentative, or vacillating.

As you know, meekness is frequently mentioned in the scriptures in various ways. Elder Maxwell described meek Moses and meek Enoch. Jesus taught clearly the special affection He reserves for the meek. Various prophets in all dispensations have linked meekness with other words that sometimes appear to be synonyms and sometimes are complementary with additional meanings. Because of your scholarship and your familiarity with these references I will not detail them further except to commend them for your pondering and consideration. In the main, meekness scriptures are found in three categories: 1) They are taught by Jesus as in the Sermon on the Mount; 2) they describe Jesus as in the Messianic references in Isaiah; and 3) they testify of Jesus or urge emulation of Him, as in King Benjamin's address.

Abinadi, in speaking to a group that I am sure considered themselves to be intellectuals, made a telling observation that deserves our consideration as we strive to meld the sacred with the secular and achieve excellence in both spheres. "Ye have not applied your *hearts* to understanding; therefore, ye have not been wise" (Mosiah 12:27, emphasis added). Note he did not say "applied your heads," or "your minds." I assume that they did not require that directive. Abinadi reminded his listeners of what we should already know: that is, reason and revelation are not opposites, they are complements. Extremist advocates for either position might reject the other, but there is no place for an exclusionary view in one who aspires to be a true disciple-scholar.

The importance of right "hearts" is repeatedly emphasized in the scriptures. To be true disciples, we need not only clean hands but pure hearts (see Psalm 24). However, even for the disciple, significant scholarship is also a requisite for success. You will recall that Elder Maxwell in his recent tutorial used Oliver Cowdery as a brief case study to illustrate this point. Remember that Oliver was not much older than most of you when he acted as scribe for the Prophet Joseph as the latter translated the Book of Mormon. Oliver Cowdery wanted to do more than that and was not only promised that it might be so but also was instructed as to how his aspirations might be accomplished. "I will tell you in your mind and in your heart, by the Holy Ghost, which shall come upon you and which shall dwell in your heart" (D&C 8:2). Unfortunately, basically faithful Oliver did not fully appreciate that the achievement of sacred things of the Spirit often requires great mental effort.

The Lord helped explain Oliver's failure at translation in this way: "Behold, you have not understood; you have supposed that I would give it unto you, when you took no thought save it was to ask me. But, behold, I say unto you, that you must study it out in your mind; then you must ask me if it be right, and if it is right I will cause that your bosom shall burn within you: therefore, you shall feel that is right." (D&C 9:7–8.) Elder Maxwell added that Oliver, wonderful as he was, lacked not only scholastic rigor; he lacked meekness as well.

One of your great privileges in the Honors Program at BYU is that you are constantly exposed to those whose hearts and heads are right and who have regularly paid the price, both spiritually and scholastically, to have their "bosoms burn" with eternal education!

Truth from Multiple Sources

No informed person would accuse Brigham Young of rejecting the role of revelation, and yet he also felt strongly about the role of scholarship in the lives of the Latter-day

Saints. He said: "It matters not what the subject be, if it tends to improve the mind, exalt the feelings, and enlarge the capacity. The truth that is in all the arts and sciences forms a part of our religion." (*Journal of Discourses* 1:335.)

Unfortunately, others may not be so gracious in their acceptance of the need for truth from multiple sources. Scholars are often criticized for their narrowness in approach or outlook. While this may be deserved, I would suggest that this limited perspective tells us more about the nature of the natural man than it does about scholarship! If you will, this could be an example of perceptions held about my own profession. "One of the things the average doctor doesn't have time to do is catch up with the things he didn't learn in school, and one of the things he didn't learn in school is the nature of human society, its purpose, its history and its needs. . . . If medicine is necessarily a mystery to the average man, nearly everything else is necessarily a mystery to the average doctor." (Milton Mayer, in Lawrence J. Peter, *Peter's Quotations: Ideas for Our Time* [New York: William Morrow and Co. Inc., 1977], p. 327.)

Fundamental differences in approaches to knowledge, understanding, and even what knowledge is do exist in secular and spiritual spheres. While these differences are usually emphasized, their similarities are more and greater than is commonly acknowledged. In science, to use the term broadly, truth is usually accepted tentatively with the expectation that we are always awaiting the "better answer." Today's theory, while perhaps the best explanation we currently have, will give way to tomorrow's hypothesis, which incorporates new data not now available.

By contrast, true disciples understand that there are absolute truths, those of highest quality as described by Elder Maxwell, that are, always have been, and always will be the correct answers. We will know more in the future than we do today about the specifics of genetic replication, but we will never need more detail about the law of chastity than we have now or indeed than was emphasized on Mount Sinai.

Learning by Study and Also by Faith

Given these stark differences in approaches to learning and knowledge, why might I suggest similarities? Because each scholar, secular or spiritual, begins her or his quest for understanding by making some basic assumptions. The scientist usually sees these assumptions as building on the discoveries and thinking of scholastic predecessors. The disciple views them as acts of faith or testimony that confirm revelation as a vital, active principle and the scriptures as true records of God's word. Both approaches begin someplace and depend on the antecedent knowledge generated by efforts of others and by means other than their own.

While Korihor-like arguments are frequently advanced by the supposedly learned on most university campuses today to counter the approaches to truth taken by the faithful, these professed dialectics are no more valid now than two thousand years ago and lead their unmeek advocates to the same dismal intellectual dead end.

Whatever one's points of view or biases are about learning, they all depend on faith or assumptions about something. If we expect to get the right answers, then that something on which we depend must be the right thing, and the right thing is the gospel of Jesus Christ, which, according to Brigham Young, "embraces every truth pertaining to mortal life—there is nothing outside the pale of it" (*Journal of Discourses* 1:336).

We are very fortunate to be here in this time and this place: In this time, because we live when the Restoration is sufficiently mature to accord us the reality of many heroes and models of successful disciple-scholars of our own dispensation for our edification and emulation. In this place, because on the Brigham Young University campus there is an unusual and perhaps unique concentration of scholar-saints who believe that their behavioral dispositions are as important as their academic expositions.

Meekness in Elder James E. Talmage

Dean Cox, in his excellent Honors Banquet remarks of two
weeks ago, made detailed reference to one of our common
heroes of the Restoration, Elder James E. Talmage. He
described "in his life the qualities of meekness, humility, and
submission to priesthood authority that Elder Maxwell indicated as characteristic of the disciple-scholar" ("Journey to
City Creek," Cox 1994). This same Elder Talmage who with
great inspiration wrote *Jesus the Christ* under the direction of
the First Presidency and also excelled as a leading geologist
and university president was, as some might describe him, his
"own man." Although he modeled meekness and his humility
was unfeigned, he also had healthy respect for his own views
and preferences and was not easily dissuaded by others. Two
interesting stories about Elder Talmage, told by his son John,
give an insightful view of Elder Talmage that make his examples of meekness, humility, and submission to priesthood
authority even more remarkable.

While serving as university president in the 1890s, Brother
Talmage obtained a bicycle, which was then the new wave in
transportation.

> James acquired one of the new machines, not as a hobby or phys-
> ical conditioner but as a practical means of transportation. . . .
>   Some time after James had achieved reasonable proficiency
> in handling his machine on standard roads, he showed up at the
> front door one evening a full hour late for dinner and scarcely
> recognizable.
>   May [his wife] nearly went into shock, for her husband was
> a frightening sight. Battered, bruised, and bleeding profusely,
> clothes torn in a dozen places and covered with dust and mud,
> James looked as though he had been caught in a riot, or at least
> a fight of unusual violence. Neither, it developed, had been the
> case.
>   Half a block from the Talmage home a single-plank foot-
> bridge crossed the ditch of running water that separated the
> street from the footpath. Until now, James had dismounted when

he reached this point in a homeward journey, and crossed the narrow bridge on foot. Today, he had decided that he had reached the point in his development as a cyclist where he should no longer resort to this prudent maneuver, but rather ride over the bridge in the manner of an accomplished veteran of the two-wheeler.

Having so decided, James approached the bridge resolutely, confident that he would negotiate the tricky passage in a manner to be proud of and to impress neighbors, if any should chance to be watching, with his skill and casual daring. He turned sharply from the road toward the bridge with scarcely any diminution of speed. The result was spectacular and observers, if any there were, must indeed have been impressed, but in a very different way from that intended. The professor's bicycle went onto the plank at an oblique angle and quickly slid off the side, throwing its rider heavily into the ditch bank.

Dazed, bruised, bleeding and humiliated, Dr. Talmage was not convinced that the difficult maneuver was beyond his skill. Rather, he was stubbornly determined to prove that he could and would master the difficulty.

For the next hour, the president of the University of Utah might have been observed trundling his bicycle fifty yards or so down the road from the bridge, mounting and riding furiously toward the plank crossing, turning onto it with grim-lipped determination—and plunging off it in a spectacular and bone-shaking crash into the rough ditchbank. Uncounted times this startling performance was repeated, but in the end mind triumphed over matter, will power over faltering reflexes, and the crossing was successfully made. Not just once, but enough times in succession to convince James that he was capable of performing the feat without mishap at any time he might desire to do so. From then on, he never again dismounted to cross the bridge, albeit he never made the crossing without experiencing deep-seated qualms which he kept carefully concealed from any who might be watching. (John R. Talmage, *The Talmage Story* [Salt Lake City: Bookcraft, 1972], pp. 138–40.)

In later years, James' long hours of work, unrelieved by periods of recreation, were cause for real concern among family, friends, and associates. President Heber J. Grant, for one, repeatedly urged Dr. Talmage to take up some form of sport, if only for its therapeutic value. Himself an enthusiastic golfer, President Grant tried to get his friend to try that sport, confident (as are all golfers) that if anyone were once thoroughly exposed to golf he would be captivated by its subtle but powerful attractions.

As President Grant's urgings increased in frequency and intensity, so did Dr. Talmage's demurrers on the grounds of lack of interest and lack of ability to master a complicated skill so late in life. President Grant was certain the skill could be mastered and that interest would automatically follow. Finally a compromise was reached, and a test agreed upon: James would give the game of golf an honest trial, and work at it until he was able to hit a drive which President Grant would rate as satisfactory, "a real golf shot."

"If you hit just one really good drive, nature will do the rest," President Grant assured his pupil-to-be. "You won't be able to resist the game after that."

It was agreed that James would make his own choice after he had acquired the skill to hit the specified shot. If he felt the fascination of the game, as President Grant was certain he would, he would take up golf and play with reasonable regularity. If, after giving the game a fair trial, James still felt no interest, President Grant would cease his efforts to get Dr. Talmage to play.

On an appointed day, the two, accompanied by a number of others of the General Authorities who played golf and who had joined the friendly argument on the side of President Grant, proceeded to Nibley Park for James' first session in what was expected to be a series of lessons.

James removed his coat and was shown how to grip the club and take his stance at the ball. The coordinated movements involved in making a golf stroke were carefully explained and then demonstrated by President Grant and by others. Finally, it came James' turn to try it himself.

What followed astonished all those who watched, and probably James himself. Instead of missing the ball completely, or weakly pushing it a few feet along the grass, James somehow managed to strike the ball cleanly and with substantial force. It took off in a fine arc and with only a minimum amount of slice.

Some who saw it described it later as "a truly magnificent drive," which was probably a considerable exaggeration. However, there was consensus that the ball went close to 200 yards and stayed in the fairway. It was a drive that would have gladdened the heart of any golfer short of the expert class, and it bordered on the phenomenal for a novice.

The spectators were momentarily struck dumb, then burst into enthusiastic applause.

"Congratulations," said President Grant, rushing forward, beaming, with outstretched hand. "That was a fine shot you will remember for the rest of your life."

"You mean *that* was a fully satisfactory golf shot?" James asked, cautiously.

"It certainly was!" said President Grant.

"Then I have fulfilled my part of the agreement?"

"You have—and don't you feel the thrill of excitement? Now you'll be playing regularly. As a matter of fact, we can go into the clubhouse now and I will help you select a set of clubs."

"Thank you," said James, putting on his coat. "If I have carried out my part of the agreement, then I shall call on you to live up to yours. You promised that if I hit a satisfactory drive and did not feel the spontaneous desire to play, you would stop urging me to do so. Now I should like to get back to the office, where I have a great deal of work waiting."

So far as is known, James never again struck a golf ball, or made the attempt. (*The Talmage Story,* pp. 226–28.)

Part of the genius of Elder Talmage as both a disciple and a scholar was the ability to separate the important from the trivial. While sensitive to the perceptions of others, at least some of the time, he was also comfortable in taking "the road less traveled." He meekly responded to authority, crisply and without reservation, when asked to prepare *Jesus the Christ* or undertake major missions, but he also could withstand social pressures from conventionally compelling sources, as his brush with the game of golf demonstrates.

Discipleship and the Things that Matter Most

That he liked bicycles and detested golf mattered little, and the basic outcome might have been the same had he played golf regularly with the Brethren and chosen to walk or ride a horse for transportation. He understood that some things such as meekness, humility, duty, solid scholarship, and responsiveness to duly constituted priesthood authority are vitally important not only to self but to the kingdom. Other things like golf, bicycles, how specifically one earns a living, what one's major is, or what color blouse or tie to wear are of significant personal interest but of no permanent or transcendent value in the greater scheme of life. It is fine to like bikes but not golf or the converse, but neither should distract or confuse us in the context of real discipleship and scholarship.

Dean Cox is a well-known and world-class ethnobotanist and I am a rheumatologist physician. While his scientific reputation is much more stellar than my own, both of us enjoy our work and feel we have made contributions to our disciplines. I suspect, however, that we will both need much more than facility in the scientific method to be successful in our new vocations in the eternities when all the answers about botany and arthritis that matter will already be available! I suspect also that no one will care much about what cars we drove or how we spent our leisure or even in what journals we published. But I believe some, particularly our families, might be impacted by our capacity to acquire some of the characteristics, like meekness, of the serious disciple.

As each of you determine your own course in the exciting challenge of developing your own productive mix of discipleship and scholarship, might I suggest you note positive examples from your own experiences and then apply them personally. You might find an experience from my own college days to be of interest.

One of the great scientist-disciples of our time was Dr. Henry Eyring, the father of Elder Eyring, our Commissioner of Education for the Church. Professor Eyring was a truly world-class chemist who was not one whit affected by the considerable honors of men that he received, and thus his scholarship never confused or compromised his discipleship.

He and I were at the University of Utah together. Dr. Eyring was Distinguished Professor of Chemistry and Dean of the Graduate School, and I was a freshman. Although we became somewhat acquainted in later years, I am sure he had no idea who I was at that time. I never had a class from him, although I had heard him speak a time or two with great admiration. I knew of his academic distinction and his gospel devotion. What really impressed me about Henry Eyring, however, related to a very brief chance encounter I had with him in the basement of the Park Building, the main administration building at the University of Utah.

We happened to arrive at the same water fountain from opposite directions at precisely the same time. Fortunately, I remembered some of the things my mother had tried to teach and I attempted to step back and defer to this older gentleman of such significant status. He would have none of it! With a twinkle in his eye and a smile he said: "Young man, please go first. I'm sure that you are busier than I am." I had a short, refreshing drink and have ever since been refreshed by the warm feelings elicited by a simple, thoughtful, generous act of meek Henry Eyring. Professor Eyring is famous for many things, but in my mind and heart I always see him at the Park Building water fountain.

In their recent presentations to you both Elder Maxwell and Dean Cox have reminded us of King Benjamin's description of what is required of us to become Saints or disciples through the atonement of Christ. The qualities of becoming as a child, submissive, meek, humble, patient, full of love and willingness to submit to all the Lord inflicts (Mosiah 3:19), are understandable for discipleship if sometimes difficult to implement. It is interesting to note, however, that while the "natural man" (an enemy to God) might well describe many scholars, enmity to the Father is *not* a characteristic of scholarship!

Discipleship and Humility

In fact, the real scholar is meek, and has much to be meek about, because she or he, like Nephi, does "not know the meaning of all things" (1 Nephi 11:17). The dictionary defines a scholar as "a learned person," and the scriptures teach that "to be learned is good if they hearken unto the counsels of God" (2 Nephi 9:29). We must remember, however, that the Lord "despiseth" those "who are puffed up because of their learning" (2 Nephi 9:42). We are to be meek and humble because we yet know so little, and yet we can appropriately be anxious in anticipation that if we prove faithful as true disciples we shall, in time, receive and know, as Jesus promises "all that my Father hath" (D&C 84:38).

To be truly meek disciple-scholars we have much to learn, but also sometimes some significant things to unlearn or forget. This is what King Benjamin refers to as putting "off the natural man." The honors of man, the vanities of the world, and the telestial temptations we all face may not be so bad in isolation but are so second-rate in comparison to what really matters most!

Someone once described his own feelings when struggling to reach new scholastic heights. "My mind is like my grandmother's attic. It is filled with things no longer useful, but too good to throw away." In my case, these sentiments may apply not only to things in my own head that are of lesser value but also to habits or traits that I seemingly hold dear, at least behaviorally, but that do not facilitate reaching the goals I have set for myself or the standards established for us by the Savior. A map of the Andes may be beautiful and interesting but it is not much help when backpacking in the Uintas. Both are wonderful mountain ranges, but what significant differences!

Similarly, the books I read, the movies I see, and even the thoughts I think may, in themselves, have some value but cannot and should not replace the scriptures, prayerful contemplation, and the counsel of our living oracles. In large part the quality of our discipleship and our scholarship will depend on what we emphasize in our lives rather than on what we wish had been our focus.

Meekness is required in spiritual as well as in secular endeavors. In President Benson's classic sermon on pride (*Ensign,* May 1986), I find no limits on the spheres to which his cautions apply. Alma taught that meekness is not only a desirable characteristic but is required by those seeking to be led by the Holy Spirit (see Alma 13:28). Mormon considered meekness to be an antecedent to the first principle, faith (Moroni 7:39)! He further wrote that none is acceptable before God save the meek and lowly. The Lord, through the Prophet Joseph, reminds us that meekness is not weakness but rather is required for us to become strong (D&C 84:106).

Elder Maxwell reminds us that "in opting for discipleship, we have nothing to fear but the disapproval of the natural man and his like-minded, preoccupied friends—with their pointing fingers" ("The Disciple-Scholar," 1994). As they point at us, we should point toward meek Jesus and learn what He has provided for us as we strive to be more like Him. Of His meekness, let me refer briefly to several episodes in His earthly ministry that are already well known to you.

Jesus as the Example of Meekness

We know that Jesus, as a youth, "grew, and waxed strong in spirit, filled with wisdom: and the grace of God was upon him" (Luke 2:40). We remember the Feast of the Passover episode when He became separated from Mary and Joseph. We can quote easily "Wist ye not that I must be about my Father's business?" (Luke 2:49), but do we also remember that "he went down with them, and *was subject unto them*" (Luke 2:51, emphasis added)? Might this be a good lesson and example for those of us who have perhaps exceeded our own parents in terms of educational opportunities and other worldly advantages but still owe them so much for so much that is most precious?

At the time Jesus was baptized He knew who He was, and yet He willingly submitted to proper priesthood authority and discipline (see Matthew 3:13–15).

As Jesus was fasting in the wilderness He encountered Satan, who tried to tempt Him, as the devil does with all of us. Meek Jesus did not brag, He did not argue, He did not perform for others. He meekly declared the truth and faithfully followed His own standard of conduct. (See Matthew 4:1–11.)

Jesus meekly responded to His critics. He was gentle but direct. When asked, "Why do ye eat and drink with publicans and sinners?" He answered, "They that are whole need not a physician; but they that are sick" (Luke 5:30–31).

Jesus advised His followers to meekly underestimate, rather than inflate, their status among others. He suggested that when invited to a dinner or wedding party they sit with the most modest of guests and wait to be invited to come higher rather than cause embarrassment for their hosts or themselves (see Luke 14:7–10).

Jesus taught with amazing patience and meekness. If anyone could be excused for self-aggrandizement, possessive pride, or the explication of complicated dogma, surely it would be the Creator of the universe under the direction of the Father. Yet that was never His style. When asked by the rich young man the key question, "What shall I do to inherit eternal life?" Jesus knew the young man's heart and his specific weaknesses and yet said, "Thou knowest the commandments" and enumerated several of the key ones. When the young man claimed lifelong compliance, Jesus pointedly but gently reminded him, "Yet lackest thou one thing." (Luke 18:18–22.) As Elder Maxwell pointed out last month, the young man lacked meekness.

Jesus' meekness brought out the beginnings of meekness in others. His demeanor and approach—patient, quiet, waiting but direct—not only saved from stoning the woman taken in adultery but also probably saved the souls of those originally intent on being rock throwers themselves (see John 8:3–11).

Jesus modestly and meekly refused to take credit for things

that rightly belonged to the Father or to others. "My doctrine is not mine, but his that sent me" (John 7:16), said Jesus. What are the lessons here for the scholar deeply drenched in the attitudes of our selfish world?

Jesus never expected more meekness from His disciples than He demonstrated Himself. He washed the feet of the Twelve with the reminder that "I have given you an example, that ye should do as I have done to you" (John 13:15).

He responded to individuals, as well as groups, in great need. After the Crucifixion and his resurrection, many of the faithful were confused and depressed and were fearful that the skeptics and critics might be right. Jesus might have majestically confronted the people, declaring His reality, but rather He meekly taught and encouraged and quietly revealed Himself to those who really cared about what had in fact happened. He had risen! You recall the wonder and thrill of the two discouraged disciples on the road to Emmaus when finally "their eyes were opened, and they knew him" (Luke 24:31).

While we, as a special academic community, strive to be both scholars and disciples of quality, we are faced with the challenges of not only the wicked world without but also the temptations and foibles of the "natural man" within. Many of the blessings of the atonement of Christ are made available unconditionally to all people, even the scoffers and critics. Yet some of the most significant blessings are reserved for those who give both allegiance and adherence to the code of discipleship outlined by the Master, Jesus Christ. When asked by one of the faithful how we might solidify our relationship with Him, "Jesus answered and said unto him, If a man love me, he will keep my words: and my Father will love him, and we will come unto him, and make our abode with him" (John 14:23).

May we meekly but energetically balance our scholarship and discipleship in ways that articulate our love for the Savior and give us the realistic hope of entering the abode of the Father and the Son is my prayer.

4

ELDER HENRY B. EYRING

Faith, Authority, and Scholarship

I am deeply grateful to be here with you this evening, and I pray that the Spirit of the Lord may be with us. I know that you had chances to be many places this evening and I'm grateful that you chose to be here. Your faith will help us all.

I learned something about the connection of faith, authority, and scholarship one night not long ago. I was in Hartford, Connecticut. I had come for a stake conference. It was scheduled in such a way that we stopped our conference meetings in the late afternoon and sat in the back of a darkened chapel to watch the Young Women satellite broadcast from Salt Lake City. The room was half-filled with teenage girls who had gathered from across that far-flung stake to be together and to be taught. It went on beautifully, at least it seemed to me. And then, near the end, Elder Dallin H. Oaks stood to speak. You won't understand my emotion now unless you can imagine what it's like to be presiding as a General Authority in a stake conference, trying with all your energy and faith to have the mantle of your call give you power beyond your own, and then to see the mantle of an Apostle on Elder Oaks. I understood, in a personal way, what the philosopher Kierkegaard meant when he said: "Genius is what it is of itself. An apostle is what he is by his divine authority."

Surrender to the Office of an Apostle

I knew I was hearing the Lord's message to me as Elder Oaks began with the words: "The first principle of the gospel is not faith. The first principle of the gospel is faith in the Lord Jesus Christ." In that moment I felt at least a double surrender. I felt a surrender to the office of an Apostle. I knew I was not hearing the words of a former university president or of a Supreme Court justice or even of a brilliant man. I did not so much see the man I have known well; rather, I heard the voice of his office, a voice of authority. And because I felt and knew the words were true, I felt another surrender of my independence. I felt myself surrender to the authority of Jesus Christ. I felt myself want to know what He would have me do.

And then I realized that the Savior Himself, the creator of the universe, described His own surrender in this way, as recorded in the Bible: "I can of mine own self do nothing: as I hear, I judge: and my judgment is just; because I seek not mine own will, but the will of the Father which hath sent me" (John 5:30).

And then again in this way in the Book of Mormon: "And behold, I am the light and the life of the world; and I have drunk out of that bitter cup which the Father hath given me, and have glorified the Father in taking upon me the sins of the world, in the which I have suffered the will of the Father in all things from the beginning" (3 Nephi 11:11).

And in this way, even later, in the Doctrine and Covenants:

"I am Jesus Christ; I came by the will of the Father, and I do his will" (D&C 19:24).

Now, you may see what appears to be a paradox. The Savior of the world, who is our perfect example in all things, including scholarship, by His own account defers to the authority of His Father. Because we have faith in Jesus Christ, we defer our will to His authority. And because we have faith in living Apostles of the Lord Jesus Christ, we defer to that authority as well. And yet here is the apparent paradox: most reviewers of any scholarly journal would ask you to edit out of an article, on pain of rejection, any reference to divine authority or to the authority of an ecclesiastical leader, either in the theory you present or in your evidence. I suppose the exception might be an article or a book in which you examined religious ideas or religious people, as long as you kept expressions of your own faith in the preface and out of your argument or evidence.

Submission to Jesus Christ:
Scholarly Burden or Strength?

The paradox the world would see is that we aspire to be the best of scholars and yet we will do it with full faith in Jesus Christ and His living servants. My message tonight is that faith in Jesus Christ, including what it requires in submission to authority held by His mortal servants, is not a burden to you as a scholar but is your strength. Let me try to tell you why and how.

We can begin best with words of Elder Neal A. Maxwell, an Apostle of Jesus Christ. In his talk to you last January 27 he said this: "To be a disciple-scholar in our time is a call to high adventure! Just as one's quest for knowledge should be unending, so, too, should the quest for greater love, meekness, and patience. In considering consecration, it is well to remember . . . that nothing is held back—whether turf, attitude, or hobbies.

One's will is to be swallowed up in the will of God—just as occurred with Jesus."

He gave a reference to Mosiah 15:7, but he didn't read it. Here is what that scripture says: "Yea, even so shall he be led, crucified, and slain, the flesh becoming subject even unto death, the will of the Son being swallowed up in the will of the Father."

Elder Maxwell then said, "Though I have spoken of the disciple-scholar, in the end all the hyphenated words come off. We are all finally disciples—men and women of Christ. But is consecration asking too much? . . . It certainly involves a submission to authority. But what an Authority!"

And he also said that night, "Most forms of holding back are rooted in pride or are prompted by the mistaken notion that somehow we are diminished by submission to God. Actually, the greater the submission, the greater the expansion!"

Submission, Expansion, and Scholarly Power

That expansion includes expanding power as a scholar. Why that is so is spelled out in some scriptures you know well. I will read them to you, with the hope that your faith will lead you to have the Holy Ghost testify to you that they are true.

> For the natural man is an enemy to God, and has been from the fall of Adam, and will be, forever and ever, unless he yields to the enticings of the Holy Spirit, and putteth off the natural man and becometh a saint through the atonement of Christ the Lord, and becometh as a child, submissive, meek, humble, patient, full of love, willing to submit to all things which the Lord seeth fit to inflict upon him, even as a child doth submit to his father (Mosiah 3:19).

> And now I would that ye should be humble, and be submissive and gentle; easy to be entreated; full of patience and long-suffering; being temperate in all things; being diligent in keeping the commandments of God at all times; asking for whatso-

ever things ye stand in need, both spiritual and temporal; always returning thanks unto God for whatsoever things you do receive.

And see that ye have faith, hope, and charity, and then ye will always abound in good works.

And may the Lord bless you, and keep your garments spotless, that ye may at last be brought to sit down with Abraham, Isaac, and Jacob, and the holy prophets who have been ever since the world began, having your garments spotless even as their garments are spotless, in the kingdom of heaven to go no more out. (Alma 7:23–25.)

Submission to the Lord's Servants

In addition to submission to the authority of Jesus Christ we are asked to be submissive to His mortal authorized servants. "Verily thus saith the Lord unto you, my servant Lyman: Your sins are forgiven you, because you have obeyed my voice in coming up hither this morning to receive counsel of him whom I have appointed. Therefore, let your soul be at rest concerning your spiritual standing, and resist no more my voice. And arise up and be more careful henceforth in observing your vows, which you have made and do make, and you shall be blessed with exceeding great blessings." (D&C 108:1.)

And you will remember that the Lord said this in section 1 of the Doctrine and Covenants, the preface to that book. "What I the Lord have spoken I have spoken, and I excuse not myself; and though the heavens and the earth pass away, my word shall not pass away, but shall all be fulfilled, whether by mine own voice or by the voice of my servants, it is the same. For behold, and lo, the Lord is God, and the Spirit beareth record, and the record is true, and the truth abideth forever and ever. Amen." (D&C 1:38–39.)

Professor James Faulconer, who is here this evening, quoted Alma when he addressed your devotional. Do you remember? "And now, he imparteth his word by angels unto men, yea, not only men but women also. Now this is not all;

little children do have words given unto them many times, which confound the wise and the learned." (Alma 32:23.) Notice that God often, perhaps most often, gives His word to us through messengers.

Frequently, what God wishes us to know squares perfectly with what we would decide is true using our reason alone. That is what you would expect, since God can only speak the truth, and reason applied correctly is one way to find truth. But Leo Strauss, in *Studies in Platonic Political Philosophies,* had it right when he saw that the prophets give us the greatest gift when they tell us truth which does not square with our reason. He said: "True prophets, regardless of whether they predict doom or salvation, predict the unexpected, the humanly unforeseeable. What would not occur to men, left to themselves, to fear or to hope."

It is crucial which of those prophetic surprises you study first. As a student of geology or biology you might start with the specifics of creation as living prophets have taught them; or as a political science major you might consider what they have said about socialism. I would urge you strongly to start somewhere else: start with the prophecies about how the gospel of Jesus Christ will change you. From that you will see why faith in Jesus Christ and in the authority of His mortal servants will multiply your scholarly powers. Then, when you have acted on that, you will be able to see how the other predictions and sayings of prophets will expand, not contract, your understanding.

Here is the place I would suggest you start. It is a prediction about the future, your future and mine. It is this: Only through submission to the restored gospel of Jesus Christ in faith will you gain eternal life; and by that submission you will gain the constant companionship of the Holy Ghost. You know the power of that promise from this scripture. "And when ye shall receive these things, I would exhort you that ye would ask God, the Eternal Father, in the name of Christ, if these things are not true; and if ye shall ask with a sincere heart, with real intent, having faith in Christ, he will manifest the truth of it unto you, by the power of the Holy Ghost. And by the power of the Holy Ghost ye may know the truth of all things." (Moroni 10:4–5.)

Christ as the Example of Submission

I can tell you best about how that voluntary submission comes by a personal story. I was listening to an Apostle speak in general conference. It was Elder Maxwell. In his address he used a visual image which carried me in my mind out of the Tabernacle, where I was sitting. He spoke of the terrible effects of sin in the world. He spoke of the abuse of children, which sometimes ends in their cruel deaths. He said that in even a short period of time the number of victims would fill a classroom. Suddenly I was transported in my mind to a classroom of children who were laughing in their innocence, and I loved them and felt pain at the thought of their being abused and perhaps killed.

But in the seconds it took that picture to form in my mind, Elder Maxwell placed another one there. It was that Jesus Christ in the garden and on the cross knew the suffering of those children, understood their anguish, knew for Himself their terrible experiences in the past and the future, knew the despicable motives of the people who would harm them, and then, out of love, paid the price for those fiendish degradations.

Even as He felt the anguish of the children, He took upon Him the pain a just God would require of the most evil of people. He understood perfectly the most despicable motives of people who did and would do such things. He felt all the terrible consequences. And then, for those perpetrators of all evil, He paid a price that no ordinary mortal could ever pay. He paid the full price of that horror. Then I tried to think of His doing that for all the cruelty and evil in the history of this earth. That's my Savior and your Savior, and that is the authority to which we submit.

In that moment of listening to an Apostle, I wanted to be a better, a more submissive, more faithful servant of Jesus Christ. I can feel what Elder Maxwell meant when he said to you in his lecture here that we must be submissive to authority, "but what an Authority!"

Now, you can see why Elder Maxwell also said that your expansion will be proportional to your degree of submission. I take that statement seriously and literally. Joseph F. Smith said it in this way: "There is no liberty that men enjoy or pretend to enjoy in the world that is not founded in the will and in the law of God, and that does not have truth for its underlying principle and foundation. It is error that makes bondsman. It is untruth that degrades mankind. It is error and the lack of knowledge of God's laws and God's will that leaves men in the world on a par with the brute creation."

Submission to Christ Is Liberating

My testimony to you is this: The effect of the Atonement is liberating and expanding. To submit in faith to Jesus Christ is liberating rather than diminishing, as the world would tell you. It is liberating because this process works: "And the first fruits of repentance is baptism; and baptism cometh by faith unto the fulfilling the commandments; and the fulfilling the commandments bringeth remission of sins; and the remission of sins bringeth meekness, and lowliness of heart; and because of meekness and lowliness of heart cometh the visitation of the Holy Ghost, which Comforter filleth with hope and perfect love, which love endureth by diligence unto prayer, until the end shall come, when all the saints shall dwell with God" (Moroni 8:25–26).

That is the "how," the description of how the liberating process of surrender works. If you exercise faith in Jesus Christ enough to desire to repent, and you're not yet a member of the Church, you'd seek for the sacrament of baptism. After baptism you will then be given the right to the companionship of the Holy Ghost. If you then live meekly and humbly enough, you will receive both forgiveness and the companionship of the Holy Ghost. And the companionship of the Holy Ghost will change you and fill you with hope and with perfect love. And I testify to you that it will bring to you the light of truth, and with that an expansion to your understanding and your capacity to feel charity, the pure love of Christ.

Submission as a Process

It is reassuring to know that this is not a one-time thing. If you live faithfully, that expansion goes on and on. And even more exciting, the power to exercise that faith increases as you make the choice in faith to submit, to obey. You will, over time, begin to lose even the desire to do evil.

You know from your experience as I know from my own that you were changed for the better in those times when you submitted to the authority of Jesus Christ. You have said, "Lord, what would you have me do?" In the mission field, it might have been to proselyte. You hit the doors. You got up at the hour the mission president asked you to get up. And in those times you have felt the Holy Ghost come to you as your companion. If you'll reflect on those times, you will also realize that your sensitivity to evil increased. The closer you drew toward God, by obeying, the more you wanted to repent and to avoid evil. The process of submission lifts you toward improvement and expansion of your mind and spirit. I testify to you that is real, not imagined.

You might reasonably ask, "But Brother Eyring, why haven't I kept on spiraling upward and been translated out of this life to a better one, if this process is so self-reinforcing?" It's because Satan knows that this process works in both directions. He knows that all he has to do is to get you to say: "Well, let's not be submissive for a while. Let's disobey."

The process works in reverse. In fact, the scriptures describe people finally becoming so hardened that they can no longer sense what they ought to be or can be. But you will not spiral downward without God reaching out to you, usually through His servants.

Submission Is Not Blind Obedience

It is terrible and wrong to speak of blind obedience, as is so often done to describe the behavior of a faithful Latter-day Saint. Rather than our being blind when we are obedient, the only time our spiritual eyes are blinded is when we are disobedient. So it's a matter of choice. We're not robots but human beings, children of our Father. Satan will pull us toward disobedience and darkness and God will send messengers to invite us to obey and to rise toward the light. But we must choose. Don't believe the lie that says that when you are submissive to God you are losing your agency. On the contrary, submission is the choice to be lifted toward the light, toward freedom, and toward expansion.

When you leave here tonight, you'll make a whole series of choices. The night is young, as they say too often. Who knows what's ahead for you? But you'll choose from many, many alternatives. You're free to choose. God made you free. He enslaves no one. He compels no one.

But after the price the Savior paid for you, won't He reach out to you? He invites. But you choose. Sitting back in your room, or wherever you are heading tonight, there are probably some scriptures. There is a floor you could kneel on. There's probably a neighbor who has some difficulties. There is probably some home teaching or visiting teaching still undone. You may have been given those assignments to care for someone else by a person of ordinary ability. You might see that God called that person and called you through him or her. So you might kneel down to see if God would have you reach out to someone for whom you are responsible. It's your choice. God won't make you do it. Your priesthood leader won't make you do it. No one is going to come and tell you to kneel down and pray and ask if there's someone who needs help. You submit as a choice. I testify to you that if you'll ask it's very likely that you'll receive an answer. If you listen, it's a still small voice.

Invite it! You'll make a choice, whether to do what the still small voice asks or not do it. How little compulsion there is in God's way! He allows earthquakes now and then. There are some compulsory means, but I try to avoid them as much as I can. He has a way to bring us to repentance, but I prefer the free-will way, as do you.

Obedience to God Lessens the Power of Evil

As you regularly choose obedience, the power of evil lessens in your life. This is the way George Q. Cannon said it: "And our minds instinctively recoil from the commission of any act which might grieve that spirit or bring a stain upon our own character or upon the divine cause in which we are engaged."

Now, once you have begun to act on your faith that Jesus is the Christ, and that His servants invite you to do His will, you will have the companionship of the Holy Ghost. That will expand your powers in the pursuit of truth because you will recognize it when you think it, read it, and hear it. But that companionship will bless you in another way. You will also come to recognize true authority, authority you can trust, and to deal wisely with authority you must examine carefully.

All your lives, people will try to assert authority over you. In your schooling, professors will profess, and they will expect you to agree with them to win their favor and to gain the rewards they have power to confer. You will have bosses who tell you what you should value in order to please them. You will have colleagues who tell you that you should do what they say, believe what they believe, because they purport to know something you don't know. You will even have public figures tell you not to follow Apostles and prophets like a sheep, but rather to follow *them.* You will have professors who are Latter-day Saints who will quote to you what appear to be contradictory statements of the Apostles and prophets to persuade you that you need not follow their counsel in that matter.

But with the Holy Ghost as your companion, none of that will swamp you. With the Holy Ghost, you will have found yourself blessed with two attributes, rarely blended in a scholar except through the fruit of gospel living. They are persistence and modesty.

Some of you have heard me tell of being in a meeting in New York as my father presented a paper at the American Chemical Society. A younger chemist popped up from the audience, interrupted, and said: "Professor Eyring, I've heard you on the other side of this question." Dad laughed and said, "Look, I've been on every side of it I can find, and I'll keep trying other sides until I finally get it figured out." And then he went on with his lecture. So much for looking as though you are always right. He was saying what any good little Mormon boy would say. It was not a personality trait of Henry Eyring. He was a practicing believer in the Lord Jesus Christ. He knew that the Savior was the only perfect chemist. That was the way Dad saw the world and his place in it. He saw himself as a child. He worked his heart out, as hard as he could work. He was willing to believe he didn't know most things. He was willing to change any idea he's ever had when he found something which seemed closer to the truth. And even when others praised his work, he always knew it was an approximation in the Lord's eyes, and so he might come at the problem again, from another direction.

With your faith, you will find yourself working harder because you have confidence that there is truth and that the Lord knows it. You will have to work hard because the truth He will reveal through His prophets to you will cover only a fraction of what you want to understand, and that will be focused mostly on the gospel of Jesus Christ. And when they do speak on something which comes close to some scholarly interest of yours you will listen very carefully, both because you have faith in their authority and because you know God would only prompt them to comment when it matters. The creation of the earth and of mankind must matter. Which forms of government we should prefer must matter. Whether abortions are performed must matter. Whether gambling is legalized must matter. So with a heart guided by the Holy Ghost you will listen carefully, ready to submit when the Spirit clarifies the message for you. And when it is not yet clear, you will be persistent in your pondering, modest in your lack of understanding, and obedient to God's authority vested in His servants.

I testify to you that God lives. Elder Maxwell, when he stood here at this podium, spoke as an Apostle of the Lord Jesus Christ. He came with authority and he spoke the truth when he said to you that the degree of your expansion will be proportional to the degree of your submission. I pray that you may not fear true authority, but seek it. Seek to submit to the authority of Jesus Christ, whom I testify to you is our Savior. He is the Mediator. He would take us to His Father if we would submit and let the Atonement transform us to become like Him and our Heavenly Father.

I pray that you may have no fear in whatever circumstances your great scholarly abilities may lead you. God loves you and knows you and will stay close to you and will expand you as you submit to the gospel of Jesus Christ, of which I testify in the name of Jesus Christ, amen.

5

JAMES S. JARDINE

Consecration and Learning

I am honored and humbled to be part of this lecture series. I was a student of Elder Maxwell's at the University of Utah, and his kindness and example have had a profound influence in my life. In my experience, notwithstanding the extraordinary faculties of his mind, Elder Maxwell's greatest qualities are those of his heart.

I have also benefitted for many years from my fellowship with Dr. Samuelson, the second speaker in this lecture series. As his counselor in a University of Utah stake I saw him consistently apply his considerable intellect to each issue and, when he had done his very best thinking, humbly turn over the decision to God.

These past few weeks I have read with appreciation the prior lectures in this series. In considering this presentation I have regretted my temporary "delusions of adequacy" in accepting this invitation. In light of these circumstances and setting, I have prayed for the Spirit in addressing this topic.

Consecration for the Glory of God

Dean Cox invited me to speak on consecration and learning. Consecration, doing things "unto the Lord," is both an attitude and an action. When we consecrate ourselves, we consciously reaffirm that our works are for His glory and not ours. We "confess . . . his hand in all" our work (D&C 59:21). We dedicate our talents, including our intellectual skills, to the building up of His kingdom. We ask to be used by Him. There is in the process of consecration a pledge and a petition: we dedicate our talents and our lives to God and pray that He will bless each of our mortal efforts to good effect and use in His cause. When we consecrate our learning, we ask not only to be "ever learning" but also to come to "the knowledge of the truth" (2 Timothy 3:7).

The ideal of seeking "learning by study and also by faith" (D&C 88:119) is honored better here than any other place I know. For those with gifts of intellect or related talents this is a rich environment in which to observe how others have consecrated such gifts and how we can do so.

For you students, your present talents and energy ensure a life with many opportunities. You will have to decide which of your talents should be nurtured and how to marshal them to render the greatest service possible to your family, your church, and your community. In pondering those questions, especially as college students, we often imagine a future life filled with momentous challenges and noteworthy personal contributions. However, for many of us life instead presents tasks and responsibilities which by secular standards seem mundane. If that is our lot, and it is a common one, it may require some adjustment to our expectations. But even if the world does not regard our work, there are other standards by which it is valued. Indeed, your greatest work may not lend itself to being listed on your resumé. And yet spiritual maturity will allow us to see what matters most.

As Latter-day Saints the answer to the question, "Why should we consecrate our study and learning?" is relatively simple. We believe knowledge to be part of a body of eternal truth whose pursuit and understanding is part of our eternal progress. If our noblest endeavor is to seek to become like God, we do so in part, but only in part, by striving to learn of the manifestations of His creations. Indeed, we have been admonished to "become acquainted with all good books, and with languages, tongues, and people" (D&C 90:15), and to obtain "knowledge of history" and of the "laws of [both] God and man" (D&C 93:53). Moreover, we have a prescribed duty to develop the gifts and talents, including intellectual gifts, bestowed on us by God. For instance, we may have been given the gift of "the word of knowledge, that all may be taught to be wise and to have knowledge" (D&C 46:18). Or we may have been given the talent of expression, that others might "believe on [our] words" (D&C 46:14). If these are our gifts, then we must develop them in order to consecrate them.

C. S. Lewis on Consecration

I would prefer to be entirely original on this topic, but for me the necessary starting point on consecrating our learning is an essay by C. S. Lewis I first read many years ago entitled "Learning in War-Time." It is probably not academically correct in this setting to summarize someone else's work, but I would like to do just that in part tonight for reasons which will surely become obvious.

The essay is actually a talk Lewis gave to students at Oxford in 1939, at the start of World War II. He addressed the question how students could proceed with a collegiate education when a great war for freedom was being fought in Europe. Lewis approached the question by looking at the analogous challenge for the Christian to be in the world but not of it:

[The Christian] must ask himself how it is right, or even psychologically possible, for creatures who are every moment advancing either to Heaven or to hell to spend any fraction of the little time allowed them in this world on such comparative trivialities as literature or art, mathematics or biology. (C. S. Lewis, "Learning in War-Time," in *The Weight of Glory and Other Addresses* [New York: Macmillan, 1965], p. 21).

Lewis goes on to explain that wartime is in one sense not extraordinary because life is never ordinary; women and men have always had to go on about the tasks of daily life while events or compelling causes swirl around them. Lewis observed about his own life:

Before I became a Christian I do not think I fully realized that one's life, after conversion, would inevitably consist in doing most of the same things one had been doing before, one hopes, in a new spirit, but still the same things (p. 23).

Lewis rejects the notion that the daily activities of life can be shelved in favor of great causes:

If you attempted . . . to suspend your whole intellectual and aesthetic activity, you would only succeed in substituting a worse cultural life for a better. You are not, in fact, going to read nothing, either in the church or in the line; if you don't read good books, you will read bad ones. If you don't go on thinking rationally, you will think irrationally. If you reject aesthetic satisfactions, you will fall into sensual satisfactions. (Pp. 23–24.)

Lewis then describes the essence of consecration:

All our merely natural activities will be accepted, if they are offered to God, even the humblest, and all of them, even the noblest, will be sinful if they are not. Christianity does not simply replace our natural life and substitute a new one; it is rather a new organization which exploits, to its own supernatural ends, these natural materials. . . . I reject at once an idea which lingers in the mind of some modern people that cultural activities are in their own right spiritual and meritorious—as though scholars and poets were intrinsically more pleasing to God than scavengers and bootblacks. . . . The work of a Beethoven and the work of a charwoman becomes spiritual on precisely the same condition, that of being offered to God, of being done humbly "as to the Lord." (Pp. 25–26.)

Having described consecration generally, Lewis warned of a special danger for the intellectual:

The intellectual life is not the only road to God, nor the safest, but we find it to be a road, and it may be the appointed road for us. Of course, it will be so only so long as we keep the impulse pure and disinterested. That is the great difficulty. As the author of the *Theologia Germanica* says, we may come to love knowledge—*our* knowing—more than the thing known: to delight not in the exercise of our talents but in the fact that they are ours, or even in the reputation they bring us. Every success in a scholar's life increases this danger. If it becomes irresistible, he must give up his scholarly work. The time for plucking out the right eye has arrived. (Pp. 27–28.)

Notwithstanding that danger, Lewis clearly saw a discipleship role for those with such intellectual gifts, a role he vigorously fulfilled for his entire adult life:

To be ignorant and simple now—not to be able to meet the enemies on their own ground—would be to throw down our weapons, and to betray our uneducated brethren who have, under God, no defense but us against the intellectual attacks of the heathen. Good philosophy must exist, if for no other reason, because bad philosophy needs to be answered. (P. 28.)

This essay is Lewis at his best—insightful, articulate, honest, submissive. It reminds us that there are pearls of great price in oyster beds other than our own.

Students and Consecration

How we consecrate ourselves—our hearts and minds and strengths—is a continuous and continuously evolving endeavor. Certain forms of consecration are relevant while you are formally a university student—for instance, developing a complementary graduate-level knowledge of the scriptures and the doctrines of the gospel. There are different forms of consecration when learning is primarily "on the job"—in the home, in the workplace, in Church work, in personal relations; where, as Elder Maxwell says, "we are each other's clinical material." I would like to suggest several ideas on how we may consecrate our intellectual talents, our learning "unto the Lord."

I can recall thinking, at the student stage of life, of consecrating my life in one grand, heroic gesture. But as life progresses, our moments for consecration are specific, finite, and simple. Given that reality, when we consecrate our learning we must not "look beyond the mark" (Jacob 4:14). We should be ready to consecrate our talents to the task at hand, whether or not it is a task we have envisioned for ourselves. Consecration is not a once-in-a-lifetime event; it is a daily devotion. As Paul says, we "die daily" in the Lord (1 Corinthians 15:31). If we have truly consecrated our learning, we will serve with "all our mind," whether it is in organizing the nursery or teaching a Gospel Doctrine class. This is not always easy. Professor Scruggs told me that when, as a relatively recent convert, he accepted a mission call, his sister sent him a poster which read, "Use me, O Lord, in Thy work, but preferably in an administrative capacity." The challenge of consecrating ourselves for less visible or "non-administrative" work increases proportionately as our own skills increase.

We must remember that the university was made for man, and not man for the university. For the educated, we may face the challenge of sustaining Church leaders who use bad grammar. Truly consecrating your learning allows you to look upon the hearts of such leaders and not on the outward appearance of their sentence structure. Our consecrated learning enables us more completely to comfort those who stand in need of comfort—whether they are learned or uneducated, successful or downtrodden, gracious or difficult.

Consecration and the Image of the Altar

We can facilitate our processes of consecration by using the powerful mental image of the altar. For the Old Testament people the altar was a physical place of sacrifice, of consecration and of worship. When we consecrate ourselves we lay our first things—our best gifts—on the altar in renewing acts of humility and worship. We identify our most cherished talents and consecrate them to God and, in doing so, we feel our devotion deepening and enriching. We can enhance these acts by visualizing laying them on the altar in our minds as we do them.

In my experience there is a dynamic principle at work: we not only sacrifice for those we love, but also we love those for whom we sacrifice. I know that Christ, who sacrificed Himself for us, loves us more than we can love Him. That principle explains a phenomenon you will come to know. I realized sometime ago that, in one sense, I love my children more than I love my parents. I felt some guilt about that conclusion until I realized that it resulted precisely because I had sacrificed for my children in ways and degrees that I had not sacrificed for my parents. And I further understood that, in the same way, my parents love me in the same unreciprocated degree, and that all parent-child relations have this nature, i.e., there is a great chain of unreciprocated love running down the generations. That unreciprocated parental love gives us a glimpse of our Heavenly Father's pure and unending love for us, His children.

Thus, one sure way to increase our love for others or other things is to sacrifice of ourselves for them. When we sacrifice our talents or our earthly or academic honors or our increasingly limited time on the altar to God, the act of sacrifice binds our hearts to Him, and we feel our love for Him increase.

When we render any service in the kingdom—be it teaching a Relief Society lesson or dry pack canning at Welfare Square— it will be of much less value to us if we only see it as a "To Do" item to be checked off in our Franklin Planner. But if we visualize ourselves laying on the altar to God our talents or our time commitment, such as in attending an inconvenient church meeting, then our sacrifice becomes personal and devotional to Him.

This point was brought home to me at the funeral of Dr. Henry Eyring, one of the most distinguished scientists in the history of the University of Utah faculty. It was reported that his bishop once tried to excuse him from going to the stake welfare farm on the ground that he had more important work to do. Dr. Eyring replied to the effect that while the farm did not need him, he needed the farm. I believe that Dr. Eyring consciously was consecrating his valuable and limited time on an altar to God.

Today we effectively construct altars in our lives by how we prioritize our daily activities. Our priorities become what we "worship." Since we love those things for which we sacrifice, if we devote, either consciously or unconsciously, our best gifts to or sacrifice too much at the altar of professional success or scholarly recognition, we will eventually come to love and be bound to that activity. I have seen a number of lawyers who came to "love the law," not because it was originally a worthy object of their affection but because they have knelt so long and with so much personal sacrifice at the altar of their profession. (See Matthew 6:19–23.)

There is another facet of the process of building altars. The writer Charles Williams observed that "we build our altars one place so that the fire can come down some place else." What Williams means, I think, is that we should not assume that we may dictate or anticipate how and when the spiritual fire comes down into our lives. For example, we may not have a spiritual experience at every sacrament meeting we attend, but if we are not attending sacrament meetings we are not likely to be taught by the Spirit elsewhere in our lives.

Thus, when we consecrate our talents on altars to God, we must be patient for Him to bless our labors in His own time and way and to tutor us in His own way.

Consecration of Our Learning

Consecration of our learning also broadens us and helps us avoid the pitfalls of narrow expertise. The Spirit is an expanding influence guiding us into "all truth" (John 16:13). I have a friend who is a wonderful architect. But that specialty is the lens through which he almost exclusively views the world. When we drive down the street together, our conversation is dominated by his constant critique of every building we pass. He sees the architecture and little else. And it has been a special burden for him not to let the contemporary meetinghouse building plans (some of which he does not admire) undermine his testimony. In one sense, he is in the prison of one idea. Because academia often makes us specialists, focusing our learning and education into expertise in a particular field, there is a special challenge not to measure life and others by that expertise alone. That does not mean that specialization should be avoided; only that we should beware of its potential to narrow us. At its best, specialization can develop gifts or talents that allow us to serve others in unique or customized ways.

In my experience, consecrating our learning is an expanding process. It allows us to make connections between our little area of learning and the vast other realms of life. Like Moses, we may simultaneously see that our knowledge, like ourselves, is "nothing" in the immensity of God's creations (see Moses 1:10) and yet know that we are truly His sons and daughters and in the similitude of His Only Begotten (see Moses 1:13).

An illustration of this expanded perspective was related by Elder Dallin H. Oaks some years ago. Between the time of his call and his starting his work as an Apostle there was one month in which he finished his work at the Utah Supreme

Court. He said that as he labored during that period to finish his work at the court, his mind would often race forward to his new responsibilities. He said that one afternoon in chambers he was contemplating his new calling when he began to think how well prepared he was for it: he had considerable public speaking experience, he was widely traveled, and he had much administrative and committee experience. He said that as that thought lingered he was suddenly struck with the insight that he was supposing that the calling was to fit him when in truth he was to fit the calling. It was, he said, both a piercing and a lasting impression.

Serving Where Called

You may find that what is asked of you will not always coincide with what you believe you have to offer. It is often the case that just when we are ready to present our talents as a Gospel Doctrine teacher, we are called as a Scoutmaster. If we have truly consecrated our talents it will not matter how we are used, but only whether we are used. Truly consecrating our talents to the Lord means submitting to His use those talents, when and how He wishes. We are told that God uses us "not according to our works but according to his own purposes" (2 Timothy 1:9). Thus when we consecrate our works we must do so to His purposes and not to our preferences.

Related to this attitude of mind is the act of acknowledging God's "hand in all things," including in our intellectual or academic successes. If our motivation is the attainment of academic or secular honors, our eye will be single to our own glory. Consecrating our intellectual talents to God moves us from dwelling on our past honors to focusing on the future work to be done. In his book, *Joseph Smith and the Beginnings of Mormonism,* Dr. Richard Bushman describes this aspect of consecration in the life of Joseph Smith. In describing the initial publication of the Book of Mormon, Dr. Bushman writes:

For all the effort and trouble he put into the translation, Joseph made little of the book's appearance. Neither he nor his mother named the day when bound copies were available or mentioned any celebration. (Perhaps Joseph was in Pennsylvania on March 26.) The first edition said virtually nothing about Joseph himself. The preface contained one sentence about his part in the work. "I would also inform you that the plates of which hath been spoken, were found in the township of Manchester, Ontario county, New York." His own name appeared only on the title page and in the testimony of the eight witnesses at the back. It was an unusually spare production, wholly lacking in signs of self-promotion. Joseph presented his handiwork to the public and moved on. The book thenceforth had a life of its own. (Pp. 112–13.)

This is a remarkable insight into the character and mission of Joseph Smith. Given his investment of time and energy in translation and the suffering associated with its publication, it is extraordinary that he did not seek personal recognition on its publication. But Joseph went on no book tour; he was busy with someone else's work.

There is a particular challenge for the learned to confess God's hand in all things. That is because one aim of our education is to make us independent, to learn skills to manage outcomes—to control our environments. In the secular world we may come so to believe in our intellectual skills that we confidently try to proceed to design our own futures. Of course, life has a habit of awakening us rudely from this naivete. When I was in law school a friend of mine was a brilliant fourth-year medical student. His earnest belief in the good he would do as a doctor was absolute. Then his wife contracted an extremely rare form of arthritis, a form theretofore diagnosed, as I recall, only six times and only in men. After three painful months in bed she recovered completely with no apparent explanation. Several weeks later my friend rose in fast and testimony meeting, specifically confessing his overconfidence in the arm of flesh and humbly acknowledging God as the great Healer.

Becoming Tools in the Lord's Hand

In consecrating our talents and learning we must avoid conditioning our consecration on the end result we want. Hopefully we learn to recognize in ourselves the human temptation to offer what a friend of mine calls the "architect's prayer"—where we pray for the blueprint and ask God to be the general contractor. Rather, instead of doing our work in His name, we must consecrate ourselves to be used by Him, whether or not we will ever know fully how we were used. Indeed, we may never know.

As a first-year law student at Harvard I was very lonely and overwhelmed. I had never before been east of Denver, I was not married, and I was living in a dorm room not more than ten by twelve feet in dimension. For the first time in my life I was studying every waking minute, weekdays as well as Saturdays. I was homesick.

One Saturday afternoon I was researching a paper in the law school library and feeling particularly low. In this state I was looking for a book in a dark corner of the fourth-floor library stacks when I saw on a shelf an old copy of the Book of Mormon. Surprised, I opened it. On its flyleaf it read, "Donated to the Harvard Law School Library by John A. Widtsoe, 1894." In that moment I felt a flood of brotherhood, of shared suffering and of common belief. A light shone in on my spirit by an act of Elder Widtsoe's done decades earlier when he was a college student at Harvard. I doubt he ever imagined that a beneficiary of his act would be another young Latter-day Saint so many years later. But he consecrated that gift without knowing, or needing to know, how God would use his offering.

When we consecrate our learning we invite the Spirit into our mental processes. As Latter-day Saints, we have special views about this. We believe the Spirit frees us from the limits of our human learning processes. Science and philosophy have come to recognize that "knowledge is tied to the conditions under which it [is] secured" (Eric Erickson, *Childhood and Society*, p. 17). Even the most objectively designed experiments and searches for knowledge inevitably are distorted by the sensory limitations and the subjective perspectives of the supervising scholars and scientists and of the limitations of the current scientific paradigms (see Thomas Kuhn, *The Structure of Scientific Revolutions*). This recognition has resulted in a humility about our scientific knowledge and its limitations. As Latter-day Saints we believe that the Spirit can lift us beyond the limitations of our senses. We are told that the Spirit enables us not to "judge after the sight of [our] eyes, neither reprove after the hearing of [our] ears" (2 Nephi 21:3). We are told in several places that by the Spirit we may know things as they "really are" (Jacob 4:13; D&C 93:24). Oliver Wendell Holmes once said that "a mind expanded by an idea can never return to its original dimension." As Latter-day Saints, we believe the Spirit expands and objectivizes our minds in the search for truth (see Alma 32:28, 34–36). By consecrating our learning we invite the Spirit to so expand us and lift us as we gain pure knowledge and truth.

There is a potential danger in devoting our learning to the work of the kingdom. This is illustrated partially by the story of a Primary class of six-year-olds in Montana. One Sunday the Primary teacher asked the class, "What is brown and furry with a big bushy tail and stores nuts for the winter?" An eager little boy on the first row raised his hand and said: "I know the answer is Jesus but it sounds like a squirrel to me." We must not be so eager in our desire to consecrate our talents that we lose sight of our goal. Lewis said: "By leading that life to the glory of God I do not, of course, mean any attempt to make our intellectual inquiries work out to edifying conclusions. That would be, as Bacon says, to offer to the author of truth the unclean sacrifice of a lie." ("Learning in War-Time," *The Weight of Glory,* p. 27.)

I was in a student stake presidency at the time when Mark Hoffman produced the so-called salamander letter. Most of you will recall Hoffman as the man who murdered two innocent people in Utah nearly a decade ago to cover up other crimes. Hoffman had forged documents relating to Church history, including one purported letter in which Joseph Smith described a white salamander as part of his visionary experiences. This letter created difficulties of explanation for Church members and even caused some to leave the Church. Because I was serving in a university stake setting, I discussed its import with a number of young Latter-day Saints. I began to try to develop various intellectual or historical explanations of the letter, including, as I recall, a reference to the French translation of the word *salamander.*

One Sunday, our stake invited Dr. Reed Durham, a faculty member at the University of Utah Institute and a wonderful scholar, to speak to our stake priesthood meeting on the letter. Because of his substantial scholarly attributes, I looked forward to Dr. Durham's presentation. But when he spoke he offered no historical or textual analyses or other explanation of the letter. Rather, his message was that we knew very little about the letter or its history, that we should seek to know more, but that having the Spirit as our guide gave us the only sure footing in that journey. He then bore his testimony of the calling of Joseph Smith and the divine origins of the Book of Mormon. Because I expected and perhaps wanted an academic approach, I was initially disappointed in his remarks. But events and subsequent reflection have shown that Dr. Durham knew well not to try to help God out with bad arguments.

If we seek truth humbly, God can use us and will use us when we are willing.

Asking God to Consecrate Our Efforts for Our Welfare

I discovered in the scriptures some years ago a particular way to consecrate my efforts. When I was a young bishop of a student ward, I felt drained by the demands of the calling. I did not so much feel out of tune as I did fatigued. I reached a point where I was heavily laden by the work of the calling and not experiencing the growth I had expected from the service.

During that time I reread 2 Nephi 32:9, which struck me with a new meaning. "But behold, I say unto you that ye must pray always, and not faint; that ye must not perform any thing unto the Lord save in the first place ye shall pray unto the Father in the name of Christ, that he will consecrate thy performance unto thee, that thy performance may be for the welfare of thy soul."

Reading that scripture I realized that my prayers had been only that the Lord would bless those I was seeking to serve. I had not prayed that He would consecrate my performance "unto me" or to ask that my efforts would bless and fill my own soul. My prayers since that time have changed. When we consecrate our efforts to the Lord, He counsels us not only to pray that others will be blessed but also to pray that we will be blessed. In the act of laying our labors on His altar, we should ask Him to consecrate our hearts and minds to our own welfare. That is not a selfish prayer; it is a submissive prayer.

Let me summarize how we may consecrate our learning.

- We can deepen the experience of devotional love by visualizing our efforts as sacrifices on the altar of God.
- We must be ready to consecrate daily the simple and even mundane labors in our lives.
- We should beware of making sacrifices at the altar of professional success or academic honor.
- When we truly consecrate our talents and our learning, we are expanded beyond our own works to fit God's purposes and lifted beyond the limitations of our senses and biases.
- When we consecrate our talents to God, we must willingly accept that He may use those talents in ways we could not have predicted and may not have chosen, had it been left to us. In particular, we must not condition our consecration on getting the end result we want.
- Finally, when we offer our talents to God in His service, we should prayerfully ask Him not only to bless those we seek to serve but to consecrate our efforts to the welfare of our own souls.

When we so consecrate our learning, in my experience, we receive spiritual tutorials. We are then "taught from on high" (D&C 43:16). These teaching moments come to us in unscheduled ways.

Shortly after I had gone back to Cambridge as a first-year law student I was invited to speak in the sacrament meeting of the University Ward. The ward met for sacrament meeting in the afternoon (this was before the three-hour block meeting format), and the Cambridge Ward building had three units meeting in it, so that each of the three afternoon sacrament meetings was timed very carefully and strictly. On this occasion three students were asked to speak for not more than fifteen minutes each. We had three weeks' notice, and so I prepared very diligently for the talk. I wrote and rewrote it and timed it until I had it down to fourteen minutes 45 seconds.

On the appointed Sunday afternoon, shortly before I was to leave for church, I knelt down in my dorm room to offer a prayer that God would bless the talk I was about to give to the benefit of those that attended. While I was praying, the thought came into my mind that one of my motives was that I wanted to impress the people who would be there. This troubled me, and so I continued to pray to try to purify my motives. However, as much as I tried, I could not seem to pray that motive away. Finally, to be on time I had to get up and leave for the meeting without resolving the issue.

At the sacrament meeting I was scheduled to be the third speaker. The first speaker, another student, stood up and began to speak. He had no notes, and his talk seemed to me to be just a stream of consciousness. He went fifteen minutes, then twenty, and finally twenty-five minutes. My muscles began to tense as I could see that we were going to have a time problem. The second student speaker, also a friend of mine, took his full fifteen minutes, leaving me five minutes. As the time contracted, I became more and more frustrated, since I had cut my talk down as tightly as I could and there clearly was not going to be enough time to give it. I felt some anger towards the first speaker, whose inconsiderate use of time seemed attributable to his lack of preparation.

At that point, as the second speaker was concluding his remarks and as my frustration was peaking, the chapel in which we were sitting suddenly began to dissolve in my mind and I felt myself lifted out of it. In what was for me a piercing tutorial, I felt asked the question why I should suppose that what I had to say was more important than what the first speaker had to say, especially when I couldn't even get my motives right. It was a humbling moment, one of many instances where I have been compelled to be humble. When my time came I struggled to the pulpit, bore my testimony, and quickly sat down. That moment has stood as a reminder to me that if we genuinely consecrate ourselves and our learning, we will receive a "higher" education.

I hope and pray that we can obtain this spirit of consecration in our lives.

In the name of Jesus Christ, amen.

6

ELDER DALLIN H. OAKS

On Learning and Becoming

I am grateful to address an audience of honor students this evening. I do so in the confident expectation that BYU students who qualify for academic honors are also specially interested and qualified in the things of the Spirit.

In inviting me to address you, Dean Paul Alan Cox suggested that I might consider speaking on "how faithful scholars who speak with the bilingual voice of both the intellect and the Spirit might best serve the kingdom as it continues to fill the earth." He explained further: "Is there a special way that we, as scholars, can utilize our talents to assist in the establishment of Zion? While an academic life itself presents no special spiritual advantages over the many other honorable professions and vocations that disciples can pursue, perhaps scholastic pursuits offer unique opportunities for service. If so, what are they and how might we best prepare ourselves to grasp these opportunities?" (Letter to Elder Dallin H. Oaks, 16 September 1994.)

Moved by that challenge, I have decided to address the special ways that scholars can help to establish Zion, but I will do so indirectly. I will discuss some general principles that apply to everyone. Scholars will have no difficulty in seeing how these principles apply to their special qualifications and responsibilities.

My topic is "On Learning and Becoming." My thesis is that whereas the world teaches us to *know* something, the gospel teaches us to *become* something, and it is far more significant to *become* than it is to *know.*

The Difference Between Testimony and Conversion

I begin by reviewing some familiar scriptures in which Jesus taught His chief Apostle the difference between testimony (to know and to declare) and conversion (to do and to become).

You will remember this teaching, recorded in the sixteenth chapter of Matthew: "When Jesus came into the coasts of Caesarea Philippi, he asked his disciples, saying, Whom do men say that I the Son of man am? And they said, Some say that thou art John the Baptist: some, Elias; and others, Jeremias, or one of the prophets. He saith unto them, But whom say ye that I am? And Simon Peter answered and said, Thou art the Christ, the Son of the living God. And Jesus answered and said unto him, Blessed art thou, Simon Barjona: for flesh and blood hath not revealed it unto thee, but my Father which is in heaven." (Matthew 16:13–17.)

Peter had a testimony of Jesus Christ. He knew that Jesus was the Christ, the Messiah, and he declared it. To testify is to know and to declare.

A short time after Peter was declared blessed for his testimony, Jesus taught His Apostles about conversion. Conversion is quite different from testimony. I read from the eighteenth chapter of Matthew. "At the same time came the disciples unto Jesus, saying, Who is the greatest in the kingdom of heaven? And Jesus called a little child unto him, and set him in the midst of them, And said, Verily I say unto you, Except ye be converted, and become as little children, ye shall not enter into the kingdom of heaven. Whosoever therefore shall humble himself as this little child, the same is greatest in the kingdom of heaven." (Matthew 18:1–4.)

Later, in an experience recorded in the twenty-second chapter of the book of Luke, the Savior confirmed this lesson on the importance of being converted. This occurred at the conclusion of the Savior's mortal ministry in the sublime instructions given at the Last Supper. "And the Lord said, Simon, Simon, behold Satan hath desired you, that he may sift the children of the kingdom as wheat. But I have prayed for you, that your faith fail not; and when you are converted strengthen your brethren." (JST Luke 22:31–32.)

In order to strengthen his brethren—to nourish and lead the flock of God—this man who had been with Jesus for over three years, who had been given the authority of the holy apostleship, who had been a valiant preacher of righteousness, and who had been declared blessed by the Master for his faith and testimony, still had to be "converted."

Conversion is obviously a great deal more than testimony.

Elder Marion G. Romney characterized conversion as "the fruit of, or the reward for, repentance and obedience." He described conversion as "an actual *change* in one's understanding of life's meaning and in his allegiance to God—in interest, in thought, and in conduct." (Conference Report, October 1963, pp. 23, 24.)

Elder Bruce R. McConkie contrasted testimony, which he called a personal revelation that Jesus Christ is the Son of God, with conversion, which he said represented a change from one state to another state, as in a laboratory process that changes sugar to starch. "The same elements are present, but there is some rearrangement so that the substance seems to be different than it previously was" ("Be Ye Converted," *BYU Speeches of the Year,* 11 February 1968, p. 10).

Scriptural Descriptions of Conversion

The scriptures are full of descriptions or allusions to conversion. One of the most prominent is the familiar reference to being "born again" (e.g., Mosiah 27:25; Alma 5:49; John 3:7; 1 Peter 1:23). Alma described this as being changed from a "carnal and fallen state, to a state of righteousness," "becom[ing]" a "new creature" (Mosiah 27:25–26). King Benjamin's hearers referred to conversion as "a mighty change in us, or in our hearts" (Mosiah 5:2). The king illustrated the importance of conversion when he taught that we must "[put] off the natural man and [become] a saint through the atonement of Christ the Lord" (Mosiah 3:19).

The Apostle Paul said that persons who have been converted "have the mind of Christ" (1 Corinthians 2:16). I understand this to mean that those who have been converted begin to see things as our Savior sees them and to hear and follow His voice instead of the voice of the world. Persons with "the mind of Christ" will do things in His way instead of by the ways of the world.

The Apostle Paul illustrated that meaning in his first letter to the Corinthians: "And I, brethren, when I came to you, came not with excellency of speech or of wisdom, declaring unto you the testimony of God. . . . And my speech and my preaching was not with enticing words of man's wisdom, but in demonstration of the Spirit and of power: that your faith should not stand in the wisdom of men, but in the power of God." (1 Corinthians 2:1, 4–5.)

How had he learned this? "God hath revealed them unto us by his Spirit," Paul explained (v. 10). The Lord's way—the way of those who have been converted—is to learn the things of God from the Spirit of God.

> For what man knoweth the things of a man, save the spirit of man which is in him? even so the things of God knoweth no man, except he has the Spirit of God (JST 1 Corinthians 2:11).
>
> Now we have received, not the spirit of the world, but the

spirit which is of God; that we might know the things that are freely given to us of God.

Which things also we speak, not in the words which man's wisdom teacheth, but which the Holy Ghost teacheth; comparing spiritual things with spiritual.

But the natural man receiveth not the things of the Spirit of God: for they are foolishness unto him: neither can he know them, because they are spiritually discerned. (1 Corinthians 2:12–14.)

Another familiar scriptural description of conversion is the reference to becoming "perfect" in Christ. Moroni declares: "Come unto Christ, and be perfected in him, and deny yourselves of all ungodliness; and if ye shall deny yourselves of all ungodliness, and love God with all your might, mind and strength, then is his grace sufficient for you, that by his grace ye may be perfect in Christ" (Moroni 10:32).

Mormon seems to have been describing this same kind of conversion or becoming when he said (echoing the words of the Apostle John): "[P]ray unto the Father with all the energy of heart, . . . that ye may become the sons of God; that when he shall appear we shall be like him, for we shall see him as he is; . . . that we may be purified even as he is pure" (Moroni 7:48).

The Savior gave His own summary to the Nephites. He told them to repent and be baptized and be sanctified by the reception of the Holy Ghost, "that ye may stand spotless before me at the last day" (3 Nephi 27:20). Then He concluded: "Therefore, what manner of men ought ye to be? Verily I say unto you, even as I am" (3 Nephi 27:27).

Conversion as a Process

In a speech given here at BYU more than a quarter century ago, Elder Bruce R. McConkie gave an important insight into the nature of conversion and how it comes about. In some few

cases, such as some miracles recorded in the scriptures, conversion is an event. But for "most people," Elder McConkie
declared, "conversion is a process; and it goes step by step,
degree by degree, level by level, from a lower state to a higher,
from grace to grace, until the time that the individual is wholly
turned to the cause of righteousness" ("Be Ye Converted,"
BYU Speeches of the Year, 11 February 1968, p. 12).

Just a few years ago President Ezra Taft Benson gave this
same explanation. For most people, becoming Christlike "is a
lifetime pursuit and very often involves growth and change
that is slow, almost imperceptible" ("A Mighty Change of
Heart," *Ensign,* October 1989, p. 5).

Conversion results from personal choices, reflected in
what we do and, more subtly, in the desires of our heart.
President Harold B. Lee described this reality when he said
that conversion is to act upon eternal truths (*Stand Ye in Holy
Places* [Salt Lake City: Deseret Book, 1974], p. 92).

Comparisons with the Scholarly World

With these gospel principles in mind, we can draw some
comparisons and contrasts with comparable concepts in the
scholarly world.

In gospel terms, *testimony* is to know and to say. The scholarly world has something precisely comparable. Though the
method of obtaining secular knowledge—through study and
reason—is somewhat more limited than the method of obtaining the spiritual knowledge that is the subject of a testimony,
the object of scholarly research is also knowledge and the
result is also declaration. In the scholarly world, a "professor"
is one who has acquired a body of knowledge and who
declares or professes it.

Scholarship focuses on improving our knowledge of the
physical world, of our bodies, and of our social interactions
and institutions. Though the scholarly focus is on knowledge,
the process of scholarship and teaching obviously contem-

plates that the learner will act upon the knowledge acquired. That expectation is more explicit in education for the professions than in education in the liberal arts, but it is present throughout.

I suggest that the expectation of modern secular education generally goes no further than enlightened behavior. The goal of that kind of education does not extend to what I have called *becoming*. This is illustrated in the fact that, in contrast to the goals of their predecessors several generations ago, most modern colleges and universities disclaim any involvement in character education or any concern with the personal moral behavior of their students.

President Ezra Taft Benson contrasted the two different approaches in this familiar description of the Lord's way and the world's way: "The Lord works from the inside out. The world works from the outside in. The world would take people out of the slums. Christ takes the slums out of people, and then they take themselves out of the slums. The world would mold men by changing their environment. Christ changes men, who then change their environment. The world would shape human behavior, but Christ can change human nature." (*Ensign,* November 1985, p. 6.)

The gospel of Jesus Christ focuses on the conversion of the individual. This kind of conversion is a spiritual experience that results from an accumulation of right choices and righteous actions, not from acquiring a quantity of information or a level of physical skills. The conversion sought by the gospel does not result from a physical event or attainment that can be measured by scientific analysis. Men and women who have been converted have become something, but it is something that cannot be measured by mortal means.

Latter-day Saints are fond of quoting the Prophet Joseph Smith's statement, "A man is saved no faster than he gets knowledge" [*Teachings of the Prophet Joseph Smith,* p. 217]. This is sometimes used to suggest that the pursuit of knowledge is, by itself, a saving activity, and that all men must learn all things in order to be saved. That was not what the Prophet said. In context, it is clear that his statement referred to a particular kind of knowledge, gained in a particular way.

In the last part of the sentence quoted above, the Prophet explains that without knowledge, a man "will be brought into captivity" by some evil spirit with "more knowledge, and consequently more power." The next sentence concludes the thought: "Hence it needs revelation to assist us, and give us knowledge of the things of God." [*Ibid.*; see also D&C 130:19.] This statement identifies the kind of knowledge that saves and the ultimate method we must follow to obtain it. (Dallin H. Oaks, *The Lord's Way* [Salt Lake City: Deseret Book, 1991], pp. 72–73.)

Learning the mysteries of God and attaining to what the apostle Paul called "the measure of the stature of the fulness of Christ" (Ephesians 4:13) requires far more than learning a specified body of facts. It requires us *to learn* certain facts, *to practice* what we have learned, and, as a result, *to become* what we, as children of God, are destined to become. . . .

In inspired words now embodied in the scriptures of the Latter-day Saints, the Prophet Joseph Smith taught that "whatever principle of intelligence we attain unto in this life, it will rise with us in the resurrection" (D&C 130:18). What is meant by *intelligence* is not mere *knowledge,* by whatever means it is acquired. This is evident from the following sentence: "And if a person gains more knowledge and intelligence in this life through his diligence and obedience than another, he will have so much the advantage in the world to come" (D&C 130:19).

Note that *intelligence* is something more than *knowledge.* And note also the implication that *knowledge* is obtained by diligence and *intelligence* is obtained by obedience. Admittedly, the two methods are not mutually exclusive. But we come close to an important mystery of the gospel when we understand that the intelligence God desires us to obtain is much more than knowledge, and it cannot be obtained without obedience and revelation. That is the Lord's way, and it is far beyond the ways of the world. (Dallin H. Oaks, *The Lord's Way,* pp. 42–43.)

The ninety-third section of the Doctrine and Covenants describes how we can come unto the Father "and in due time receive of his fulness" (v. 19). The process is for a person to "keep [the] commandments" and "receive grace for grace" (v. 20) until he or she "is glorified in truth and knoweth all things" (v. 28). The acquisition of knowledge by obedience and faith is surely a different process than the acquisition of knowledge by study!

The Apostle John spoke of the ultimate conversion when he said: "Beloved, now are we the sons of God, and it doth not yet appear what we shall be; but we know that, when he shall appear, we shall be like him; for we shall see him as he is" (1 John 3:2).

Modern revelation refers to this as receiving the fulness of the Father (see D&C 76:56) and as being "gods" (D&C 76:58; 132:20).

Testimony and Conversion in Latter-day Saint Scholars

What do these principles and promises mean to Latter-day Saint scholars?

As noted, the modern objectives of what we call secular education all concern a body of knowledge—to teach it in the classroom and to enlarge it in scholarly pursuits. At Brigham Young University we have a larger mission, which makes us an object of ridicule or pity from those who do not share our vision. Those whose campus is the "great and spacious building" are frequently in the posture of "mocking" and "scoffing" at those who seek to partake of the fruit of the tree of life (see 1 Nephi 8:26–28). This is just one consequence of the reality that the world's way is different from the Lord's way.

In addition to our concern with *learning,* Brigham Young University is also concerned with *becoming,* with the *conversion* of students and also of teachers. I described my vision of that mission in an inaugural address on this campus almost a quarter century ago. "Our reason for *being* is to be a university," I said. For many, then and now, that is enough, but that is only the element comparable to testimony—to know and to declare. That is blessed but it is insufficient for those like you and me and the Apostle Peter who have been given a more comprehensive challenge than the acquisition and declaration of knowledge. And so I continued: "But our reason for *being a university* is to encourage and prepare young men and women to rise to their full spiritual potential as sons and daughters of God." (Dallin H. Oaks, Inaugural Address, Brigham Young University, 12 November 1971.) That was my 1971 description of conversion.

Almost a quarter century later we heard the same thought expressed at another inauguration. These are the words of President Howard W. Hunter giving the formal charge to the new president of BYU-Hawaii in November 1994:

> We charge you, therefore, to keep the building of character a central educational purpose of this institution. . . .
>
> [A]s you find ways to build character, you will change individuals, families, communities, and nations for the better.
>
> Finally, and most important, we charge you to build faith in God the Eternal Father, in his Beloved Son, Jesus Christ, and in the great principles which lead to eternal life, which come to us from prophets of God, both anciently and in our own time. We charge you to do that as a central part of your educational purpose, not as an addendum to it.
>
> It is the light from heaven which will make students better learners. It is the light from heaven which will make them better people—more loving, more tolerant, more productive, more honest, and thus better citizens of a community. Your students can reach their potential as learners and as human beings only as they learn to let faith in divine truth animate their whole lives. We charge you to find even better ways to invite all who study and serve here to allow this unwavering faith to rule and lift their lives. (*Profile Magazine,* December 1994, p. 15.)

With prophetic vision President Hunter reminded all of us that the principles of the gospel of Jesus Christ are more significant than the curriculum of any university. And the mission of the gospel (and in this sense the highest mission of Brigham Young University) is not just to enlarge what we *know,* but to change what we *are.* That truth poses a special challenge to scholars. Those whose professional preoccupation is the acquisition of knowledge can be quite resistant to the idea that there is something infinitely more important than knowing. Latter-day Saints who have chosen the pursuits of scholarship need an extra measure of humility to keep their talents and occupations and honors in perspective and to move faithfully and steadily toward that status of being that we call eternal life, which is the greatest of all the gifts of God. That we all may do so is my fervent prayer, in the name of Jesus Christ, amen.

Biographical Sketches of the Lecturers

ELDER NEAL A. MAXWELL is a member of the Quorum of the Twelve Apostles of The Church of Jesus Christ of Latter-day Saints. He previously served in the Presidency of the First Quorum of the Seventy and as a Commissioner of Education for the Church. Prior to his call as a General Authority he served as Executive Vice President of the University of Utah, where he held a variety of teaching and administrative assignments. He received his B.S. and M.S. in Political Science from the University of Utah and has been awarded honorary doctorate degrees from four different institutions. He has written twenty-four books on religious topics and a variety of articles on politics and government.

PAUL ALAN COX is Dean of General Education and Honors and Professor of Botany at Brigham Young University. He received his B.S. degree in Botany from BYU., an M.Sc. in ecology from the University of Wales, and an A.M. and Ph.D. in biology from Harvard University. Prior to joining the BYU faculty, he was Miller Fellow at the Miller Institute for Basic Research in Science at the University of California, Berkeley. He has written two books and over eighty articles on scientific topics.

ELDER CECIL O. SAMUELSON is a member of the First Quorum of the Seventy of The Church of Jesus Christ of Latter-day Saints. Prior to his call as a General Authority he served as Senior Vice President for Medical Affairs of Intermountain Health Care. He previously served as Vice President for Health Services, Dean of the Medical School, and Professor of Internal Medicine at the University of Utah. He received his B.S., M.S., and M.D. degrees from the University of Utah. He is a recipient of the Hans Schniff Award in Clinical Medicine at Duke University and was chosen as Outstanding Professor at the University of Utah Medical School. He has authored numerous papers on medical topics.

ELDER HENRY B. EYRING is a member of the Quorum of the Twelve Apostles of The Church of Jesus Christ of Latter-day Saints and currently serves as Commissioner of Education for the Church Educational System. He previously served as a member of the First Quorum of the Seventy and in the Presiding Bishopric. Prior to his call as a General Authority he was President of Ricks College. He was a professor at Stanford University and Sloan Visiting Fellow at the Massachusetts Institute of Technology. He holds a B.S. degree in physics from the University of Utah and received M.B.A. and D.B.A. degrees in business administration from Harvard University.

JAMES S. JARDINE is Managing Director of Ray, Quinney & Nebeker and serves as chairman of the Board of Trustees of the University of Utah. He received his B.A. from the University of Utah and the J.D. degree from Harvard Law School. He served as a White House Fellow and as a special assistant to United States Attorney General Griffin Bell. He has taught law at the University of Utah and Brigham Young University. He serves as General Counsel to the Salt Lake Olympic Winter Games Committee and has served on the Executive Committee of Utah Citizens Against Parimutuel Gambling.

ELDER DALLIN H. OAKS is a member of the Quorum of the Twelve Apostles of The Church of Jesus Christ of Latter-day Saints. Prior to his call as a General Authority he served as a justice of the Utah Supreme Court. After receiving his B.S. degree from BYU and his J.D. from the University of Chicago, he clerked for Chief Justice Earl Warren of the United States Supreme Court. He has been a professor at the University of Chicago Law School and President of Brigham Young University. He has authored nine books and over a hundred articles on religious and legal topics.

Index